Tools
for Life

DR KIRREN SCHNACK

Tools for Life

10 Essential Therapy Skills Everyone Should Know

BLUEBIRD

First published 2026 by Bluebird
an imprint of Pan Macmillan
The Smithson, 6 Briset Street, London EC1M 5NR
EU representative: Macmillan Publishers Ireland Ltd, 1st Floor,
The Liffey Trust Centre, 117–126 Sheriff Street Upper,
Dublin 1 D01 YC43
Associated companies throughout the world

HB ISBN 978-1-0350-4869-4
TPB ISBN 978-1-0350-4870-0

Copyright © Dr Kirren Schnack 2026

The right of Dr Kirren Schnack to be identified as the
author of this work has been asserted in accordance with
the Copyright, Designs and Patents Act 1988.

All rights reserved. No part of this publication may be reproduced, stored in a retrieval system, or transmitted, in any form, or by any means (including, without limitation, electronic, mechanical, photocopying, recording or otherwise) without the prior written permission of the publisher.

Pan Macmillan does not have any control over, or any responsibility for, any author or third-party websites (including, without limitation, URLs, emails and QR codes) referred to in or on this book.

1 3 5 7 9 8 6 4 2

A CIP catalogue record for this book is available from the British Library.

Typeset in ITC Galliard Pro by Six Red Marbles UK, Thetford, Norfolk
Printed and bound in the UK using 100% Renewable Electricity by CPI Group (UK) Ltd

This book is sold subject to the condition that it shall not, by way of trade or otherwise, be lent, hired out, or otherwise circulated without the publisher's prior consent in any form of binding or cover other than that in which it is published and without a similar condition including this condition being imposed on the subsequent purchaser. The publisher does not authorize the use or reproduction of any part of this book in any manner for the purpose of training artificial intelligence technologies or systems. The publisher expressly reserves this book from the Text and Data Mining exception in accordance with Article 4(3) of the European Union Digital Single Market Directive 2019/790.

Visit **www.panmacmillan.com/bluebird** to read more about
all our books and to buy them.

To my children. For all the moments we've shared, and for every moment yet to be. My love for you is endless.

Disclaimer

This book is for general information and educational purposes only and does not constitute medical, health or mental health advice. It is not a substitute for professional psychological help or therapy. It does not address individual circumstances and as such does not create a psychologist–client relationship. Readers are advised to consult their own licensed medical and or mental health advisors whose responsibility it is to determine appropriate intervention. Any reliance on the information contained in this book is at your own risk. All personal stories and examples are either anonymized or are composites to protect privacy.

Contents

Introduction 1

Part One: How You've Become Who You Are 5

1: How Genetics, Temperament and Personality Shape You 7
2: How Attachment Shapes You 13
3: How Parenting Shapes You 18
4: How People and Culture Shape You 23
5: How Trauma Can Shape You 27

Part Two: Find Yourself Through Your Values 33

1: What Are Values 37
2: Why Values Matter So Much 39
3: How to Define Your Values 41
4: How to Live by Your Values 46
5: Staying on Track 52

Part Three: Freedom from the Fear of Rejection 55

1: What Is Fear of Rejection? 59
2: What Causes Fear of Rejection? 64
3: Break Free from the Fear of Rejection 66

Part Four: Protecting Your Peace with Boundaries 85

   1: What Are Boundaries? 87
   2: Why Setting Boundaries Feels So Hard 89
   3: The Cost of Living Without Boundaries 92
   4: How to Define and Set Your Boundaries 95
   5: People's Reactions to Your Boundaries 109

Part Five: Assertiveness 115

   1: What Is Assertiveness? 117
   2: Why Does Being Assertive Feel So Hard? 119
   3: How to Be Assertive 121

Part Six: How You Stop People-Pleasing 137

   1: What Is People-Pleasing? 139
   2: Why You're a People-Pleaser 142
   3: The Price You Pay for People-Pleasing 148
   4: How to Stop Being a People-Pleaser 150
   5: What Happens When You Stop People-Pleasing 163

Part Seven: How to Deal with Conflict 167

   1: What Is Conflict? 169
   2: Why Conflict Feels So Overwhelming 171
   3: Handling Conflict with Confidence 175

Part Eight: Letting Go of Unhealthy Comparison 189

   1: What Is Self-Comparison? 191
   2: Why You Compare Yourself 192
   3: The Cost of Unhealthy Comparison 195
   4: Choosing Healthy Self-Comparison 199

Part Nine: Protecting Yourself from Toxic Behaviour 217

1: The Gut-Punch Moment 221
2: Why Do They Do It? 223
3: Do They Know They're Doing It? 225
4: Is It Them, Or Is It Me? 227
5: The Toxic Behaviours 230
6: The Second-Chance Checklist 253
7: Moving On with Clarity and Compassion 255

Part Ten: Healing from the Pain Caused by Others 259

1: Understand the Roots of Your Pain 261
2: Process Your Emotions 264
3: Taking the Power out of Painful Thoughts 266
4: Take Back the Wheel 270
5: What to Do When You Can't Move On 273
6: Forgiveness Is About You, Not Them 287
7: Getting Closure 291

An Ending and a Beginning 295
References 297
Index 305
Acknowledgements 315

Introduction

There are tools that can change your life. They're made up of therapy skills that help you through whatever's been hard. They're here in these pages, and I'm offering them to you with warmth, care and respect for whatever you've been through.

For most of us, the hardest struggles live quietly inside. But over time, they start to ripple outward, shaping how you feel, how you show up and how you handle the people and situations you face in life. Those struggles might come from that quiet inner voice – the one that whispers you're not enough, or keeps bringing up old pain, or casts a future filled with doubt. It might be the weight of self-criticism, unfair expectations, unhealthy comparison or the pressure to meet everyone else's needs. It might be that you've been pushed to your limit – by others, by pressure or by patterns that you're tired of repeating. Or maybe, you sense that something isn't right, and you're ready to stop pretending it is.

These feelings can be heavy, but they also open a door. I know how common these struggles are, and that's why I wrote this book, to help you take charge of your inner world. At its heart, it's a practical guide, full of therapy tools and psychological skills that give you something solid to hold onto when life feels overwhelming. So, wherever you are right now, this book is a space to pause. A moment to sit quietly, like you would with a friend, and gently untangle the knots that have formed over time. It's an invitation to reconnect with yourself, to understand your inner world, and come back to who you already are. So that you can start to live life with more intention, clarity and care for yourself.

I've spent more than twenty years working as a psychologist. Pretty early on, I began to notice consistent patterns – ten themes that kept showing up in what people shared with me and in what I observed. These weren't random or surface-level issues. They were, and still are, the places where so many of us get lost: how we see ourselves, how we choose our path, how we show up with others, how we hold onto ourselves, and what really matters through it all. That's how this book is shaped: ten areas that influence everything else. Ten emotional landmarks that help you live with more understanding, compassion, intention and genuine connection. It's around these that I've built your *Tools for Life*. Once you learn them, you can carry them with you forever. They'll help you with all those parts of being human you can't avoid. You can't escape yourself, and you can't escape other people, so the most empowering thing you can do is learn to live with both in a way that feels right for you.

This book begins where everything begins – with how you see yourself. Because who you are, and the story you carry about yourself, colours everything. Then we'll move into how you define your path – your identity, your values – the inner compass that helps you walk in the direction that's actually yours. From there, we'll look at how you can stop fearing rejection. How to set healthy boundaries that protect your energy and peace. How to speak up, even when it feels uncomfortable. We'll look at the pull to people-please, the gnawing guilt that creeps in when you say no, and how to gently step out of it. We'll talk about conflict, and how to navigate it without losing yourself. We'll unravel the grip of unhealthy comparison and the quiet envy it brings into your life, so that instead of feeling stuck or small, you can feel inspired to grow and make the changes you want. You'll learn how to protect yourself from harmful, toxic behaviours others might throw your way, and how to begin healing when you've been hurt by others. Whether the pain was inflicted intentionally or the lingering ache of unreturned feelings, the kind that brings longing and limerence, you'll find ways to move forward with closure and self-respect. Without tending to these ten core areas, it's easy to lose your way. Sometimes you end up building walls where you want open doors, suppressing your voice when it matters most or mistaking manipulation for love and care. You might never truly know or value the incredible person you are, someone who can live life on their own terms.

It's natural to feel that the path to change is out of reach, especially when life has left deep marks. So many people ask me if we're the way we are because we're all traumatized, as if that means we're stuck and there's no hope for change. And it's true that for many of us, life does leave its mark in some way. But what I know for sure is that you're not broken, and you're definitely not beyond change. The patterns you're stuck in may not be your fault, but they are your responsibility to change, especially if they're causing you pain. Regardless of what's happened in your past, you can create the life you want. You're not locked into an old blueprint, and you're not defined by the hardest parts of your story. Our brains – and our hearts – have this incredible capacity to change. With the right kind of guidance, self-awareness and experiences you can reshape how you are. Yes, it takes work and it takes time. But it is absolutely achievable. I've poured everything into making this guidance as accessible as possible, because you deserve the chance to reshape your life in the ways that matter to you. I know not everyone gets the opportunity to sit with a clinical psychologist. Therapy can be hard to access, whether it's navigating health system criteria or the cost of going private. That's exactly why I wrote this book: to offer you the expertise you deserve, bringing evidence-based psychology and meaningful insight, free from those barriers and here for you when it matters most.

Understanding is the first step to change. The next is gentle, consistent practice. That's why I've filled these pages with meaningful exercises; they'll help you turn insight into change and bring you closer to where you want to be. It's a great idea to have a journal or digital notepad ready to jot down your thoughts, feelings, reflections, breakthroughs and the actionable steps you'll take as you forge a new path forward to reshape the way you relate to yourself and others. You don't have to read this book in a straight line from start to finish. You might skip to the parts you need most. You might sit with a chapter for a while, or skim through one and come back for more later. You might read it all at once, and even come back to read it all again. There's no right way to walk this journey, so go with what feels best for you. Let's begin – from wherever you are right now . . .

Part One

How You've Become Who You Are

Change begins with awareness, noticing what's been shaping you, and how it's made you who you are. That's where our exploration begins, by looking inward. Reflecting on who you are and how you came to be that way. Because none of it is by accident. Your genetics, your temperament, your personality. How you were raised. The culture you grew up in. Your attachment style. And your life experiences, the highs, the lows, the hurts, the opportunities you had or didn't have. All of it has left a unique mark, some of it in ways you might not even realize. In the chapters ahead, I'll walk you through these influences one by one. Each one helping you piece together a clearer understanding of yourself. We'll start with the very first influence: the biological roots of temperament and personality, and how genetic wiring shapes us from the very beginning.

Chapter 1: How Genetics, Temperament and Personality Shape You

We all come into this world wired in our unique way; this is our temperament. It's the natural way you respond to things, and it's the patterns that have been there since you were a baby. It shapes the way you learn, interact with others and process emotions. Temperament is shaped by a mix of genetics, your environment, how you've been treated and the experiences you've had in life. Personality builds on the foundation of temperament, it's a more detailed picture of who you are, your thoughts, feelings and behaviours, your unique way of being. Personality grows and changes over time, again shaped by many things, such as your upbringing, relationships, culture and any experiences that have left their mark on you. You can think of it like a garden: the soil is your temperament, the seeds are your experiences, and together they grow into your personality.

Even though temperament is partly genetically determined and informs personality, neither is completely fixed. We often think of genetics as the concrete blueprint for who we are, that we're just stuck with it, but it's actually more complicated than that. Earlier ideas that linked specific traits to single genes are now considered overly simplistic. Research has found that it's not just one gene influencing personality traits but a whole network of genes working together.[1] This mixed effect makes it difficult to pinpoint exactly how genetics shape who we are. Research has also confirmed that genes don't just work alone; how they're expressed is influenced by the environment we grow up in, our experiences and our relationships.[2] Our environment can influence the way our genes are expressed through a process known as epigenetics, with both positive and negative experiences influencing how our genes work.[3] For instance, supportive and nurturing experiences can influence gene expression in ways that strengthen your ability to grow and adapt. On the other hand, stressful experiences can leave a different imprint, shaping how you respond to challenges. When these influences continue over time, they can lead to lasting changes in how genes are expressed, shifting the way we experience and respond to the world around us. This process of epigenetics shows how nature and nurture are constantly working together, reminding us that who we are is not set in stone.

So why am I telling you all this? Because it opens the door to a more empowering view of personal growth. This potential for transformation is at the heart of this book. Understanding this ability to transform is key to everything. As a human being how you are isn't fixed, you have the ability to change and adapt, not just in your behaviour, but in who you are at your core, and how you live your life. You've probably come across someone you haven't seen in a while and been struck by how much they've changed. Or maybe you've felt it in yourself or had someone point out that you're not the same person you used to be. My bet is these changes weren't accidental, they've grown out of everything you've lived through. And this is exactly what I'm talking about, the remarkable adaptability we have as humans to change and grow. We're always evolving and growing based on what life throws our way, what we take from that and how much we take care of ourselves.

We all change through life, sometimes slowly, sometimes quickly, and sometimes in ways we don't notice until much later. And it's often those very changes that make people stop and ask, 'Who am I?' or 'What's my real personality?' It's such a natural question. Especially when you've been through a lot, or you no longer feel like the person you used to be. We've all seen the online quizzes or the 'put a finger down' videos on social media that claim to tell you your personality. But as a clinician, I can tell you that identifying personality is much more complex than that. It involves an in-depth analysis of a person's life history, relationships, behaviour patterns and psychometric testing, often done over multiple sessions. All of that is then pulled together to identify personality traits, styles, patterns or even a possible personality disorder. This book isn't about that kind of formal assessment though. It's not about labels or fitting yourself into a box or judging yourself. It's about awareness. A starting point for self-reflection. So, below you'll find a general list of personality traits, grouped by thoughts, feelings, actions and relationship patterns. Just reflect on what resonates with you, and how these traits show up in your life. This is simply a way to notice what's there, it's not to define you in any fixed way, but to help you get to know yourself better.

How you think

Creative: You have a natural ability to think outside the box and come up with unique ideas.

Reflective: You take time to think about your experiences and what they teach you.

Self-aware: You're in tune with your own emotions and behaviours, knowing what drives you and where you can grow.

Open-minded: You're willing to consider new ideas and viewpoints without judgement.

Versatile: You have a broad range of skills and can easily switch between different things.

Pragmatic: You take a practical, no-nonsense approach to problems and focus on things that work.

Analytical: You approach problems systematically and logically, seeking clarity.

Spontaneous: You enjoy acting on impulse and embracing the moment without too much planning.

Inquisitive: You have a curious mind and like to ask questions and learn new things.

How you feel

Persistent: You keep going, even when things get tough, and are determined to reach your goals.

Optimistic: You have a positive attitude and believe in good things happening.

Patient: You have a calm and composed attitude, even when things take longer than expected.

Resilient: You're able to bounce back from challenges and work through them when things get tough.

Courageous: You face your fears head-on and are willing to take risks when you need to.

Grateful: You appreciate what you have and express thankfulness for the little things in life.

Joyful: You find happiness in everyday moments and share that joy with others.

Calm: You have a peaceful, composed presence, even in stressful situations.

Stoic: You remain strong and calm, even during difficult or painful experiences.

Reserved: You tend to keep your emotions and thoughts private and are cautious about people.

Neurotic: You experience intense emotions, worry a lot and doubt yourself, especially in stressful situations.

How you act

Adaptable: You find it easy to adapt to new situations and changes in your life.

Flexible: You can go with the flow and are comfortable making changes when necessary.

Disciplined: You have self-control and stick to your goals, maintaining focus and commitment.

Independent: You enjoy doing things on your own and are self-sufficient in many areas of your life.

Sincere: You're genuine in your words and actions and express yourself honestly.

Dynamic: You're full of energy and thrive in situations where change and action are common.

Resolute: When you make a decision, you're firm in your choices and stand by them, no matter what.

Assertive: You're comfortable expressing your thoughts and needs confidently.

How you relate to others

Empathetic: You have a deep understanding of how others feel and can easily connect with their emotions.

Tolerant: You're open-minded and accepting of different views and ways of life.

Humble: You're modest and appreciate the efforts of others, not seeking the spotlight for yourself.

Sociable: You enjoy connecting with others and feel energized by social interactions.

Agreeable: You have a warm, friendly and cooperative way with others.

Extroverted: You're outgoing, confident and interactive in social settings, and enjoy being around people.

Charismatic: You naturally attract people with your charm.

Loyal: You stand by those you care about, showing support and commitment.

Gracious: You show kindness and politeness in all your interactions, making others feel valued.

Altruistic: You care deeply about others and feel a strong desire to help and support them.

Chapter 2: How Attachment Shapes You

Attachment is the psychological bond you form as a baby, with the people who care for you in your early years of life. The attachment style that's formed then influences your later relationships, emotional responses, personality traits and resilience. Attachment theory was first developed by John Bowlby, a British psychiatrist and psychoanalyst, and was later expanded by developmental psychologist Mary Ainsworth. Their research helped us understand how important those early relationships are.[4] Attachment is built on three main ideas:

1. **We're wired for connection** – from the moment we're born, we instinctively look for someone to connect with to help us feel safe and cared for.

2. **Our early experiences create mental maps** – from these, we learn how relationships work, how we expect to be treated and how to treat and interact with others.

3. **A strong, safe bond builds confidence** – when we feel secure and supported, we're more likely to feel brave enough to try new things, trust people and handle the challenges of life.

Attachment theory suggests that we all develop one of four primary attachment styles. One of these is secure, while the other three are insecure. Studies differ in their findings, but on average, it's reported that around 51.6% of people have a secure attachment, while approximately 48.4% fall into the insecure attachment category, which includes avoidant, anxious/resistant and disorganized types.[5] But here's the part I really want you to know: attachment style isn't fixed. Even if right now you relate more to an insecure attachment style, it's entirely possible to move towards a more secure one. This shift is known as earned-secure attachment, and you'll learn more about this as you read on. This isn't a fifth attachment style, but more like a shift into feeling secure after starting out insecure. As you read through these attachment styles, take note of the one that resonates with you the most.

Secure attachment

A secure attachment is the healthiest form of attachment; it's when you feel safe and comfortable with your caregivers, you trust them and you know you're loved and cherished by them. You navigate relationships feeling safe, understood and valued. You have emotional intelligence and empathy, and you can set boundaries. You're comfortable seeking comfort; you understand yourself and others. And you can balance assertiveness with affection. And because of all this, you tend to have the meaningful relationships that we all crave. You might hold beliefs like 'I can comfort myself' and 'I am worthy of love and support'.

Anxious attachment

An anxious attachment happens when the attention and care you needed wasn't always provided, it was inconsistent, sometimes you got it, other times you didn't. When care feels off and on like this, you long for closeness, but you're also scared it won't last. Because of this, trust and feeling safe emotionally in friendships and relationships can be very fragile. You can be anxious about how you should behave with others, because you fear that you might push them away. You might over analyse your interactions, wondering if you said or did something 'wrong' that might make the other person not like you. You might be a people-pleaser, hold back when you want to speak up, or put your own needs aside just to keep others consistent and caring towards you. You might hold beliefs like 'I feel like they don't really care' and 'They'll find someone better than me.'

Avoidant attachment

An avoidant attachment develops when those who are supposed to comfort you are emotionally distant and unresponsive, especially when you're in distress and need comfort. When you have an attachment like this, you learn that trying to get help and support is pointless and that your needs are just going to be ignored. The need for connection doesn't just vanish, though; it's still there. But you learn to stop expecting your needs to be met; you might shut down emotionally, have a strong desire for independence and choose to depend on yourself instead of others. You might also build walls around yourself, pushing others away or keeping them at a safe distance to protect yourself from the disappointment of more unmet needs. You might hold beliefs like 'I don't need anyone' and 'I can handle things way better on my own'.

Earned-secure attachment

The earned-secure attachment fills me with hope, and I'm sure it will you too as you read on. Earned-secure attachment can develop after experiencing early insecure attachments. Even if you started out with insecure attachments, it's possible to grow into a more secure way of relating.

With insight, time, effort, positive relationships, meaningful experiences, and the personal growth we'll explore throughout this book, you can change things for yourself. Over time, this attachment ends up looking and feeling a lot like a secure attachment. Earned-secure attachment is the result of you finding your own way to a more secure, healthy place later in life, by making sense of your experiences, noticing how you relate to yourself and others, and gradually developing new, healthier ways of connecting with others. It's called 'earned' because it comes from the effort you've put in, the reflection and growth that helped you get there. You've earned it through what you did.

When you reach earned-secure attachment, you develop a more stable and positive sense of self. You get better at understanding and caring for yourself and others. You learn to recognize when a situation or person is healthy and safe and also spot when it's not. Your relationships feel more secure, and you're comfortable being open. You find a good balance between closeness and being independent. You feel more content, and your mental health improves.

You can also make sense of your past experiences more clearly, because they no longer have the same deep sting in them. That doesn't mean those memories suddenly disappear or that the emotions are gone; they're still there, and they might still carry some sadness or pain. But over time, they become more processed, and things feel easier. It's not that everything's suddenly perfect or that all your struggles vanish. It's just that the insecurity from your early attachment no longer has the same hold over you. It no longer creates the same kind of chaos or problems in your life. You've learned to manage it, and it no longer drives the same reactions it once did.

Over my twenty-plus-year career, I've had the privilege of witnessing countless people go through this extraordinary transformation, that has research backing it up![6] Earned-secure attachment is one of the most powerful reminders that change is always possible, even if your journey in life hasn't been easy.

Chapter 3:
How Parenting Shapes You

Parenting shapes you in ways that are different from attachment. Attachment is about the emotional bonds you form with your caregivers; parenting is about the specific ways in which you were raised. It includes the rules you had or didn't, the expectations placed on you, and the kind of guidance you were or weren't given. There are four main parenting styles: authoritative, authoritarian, permissive and uninvolved, and each leaves its unique mark.

Even though most parents usually lean towards one parenting style, they're not always a hundred per cent tied to it. Certain circumstances can sometimes cause small shifts in their approach, where they blend elements of other styles, most often authoritative, authoritarian and permissive. For instance, an authoritative parent might be more permissive in some situations, giving more freedom and choice, but become firmer when they think more discipline is needed. Authoritarian parents, though typically strict and controlling, may sometimes allow some leniency or flexibility in certain situations. And permissive parents might show some firmness when it comes to things they care deeply about. However, the uninvolved parenting style is often the most consistent one and is usually not combined with any of the other styles, because it lacks responsiveness altogether.

Authoritative parenting – balancing love, limits and growth

Authoritative parenting is seen as the most effective way to raise children, and it's often considered the gold standard. Authoritative parenting is full of love, care, warmth and responsiveness. Children have a respectful relationship with their parents, who are a dependable source of help and support. These parents are a steady hand that guides rather than controls. They set clear boundaries, explaining why they matter. Open communication means children know they are heard and valued. It teaches children to think for themselves, not just follow orders, by helping them develop problem-solving skills. This type of parenting is about learning, with parents acting like mentors. They help children understand the reasons behind expectations, rules or why particular behaviours matter. Yes, there's discipline, but it isn't about punishment; it's about teaching. Another aim of this parenting style is to help children develop critical thinking abilities that promote independence, and help children make carefully considered choices. This type of parenting helps children to become well-balanced, confident adults who communicate well, set healthy boundaries and have the resilience to deal with all of life's challenges.

Authoritarian parenting – the control-based approach

Authoritarian parenting might sound similar to authoritative, but it's completely different. Authoritarian parenting has strict rules, high expectations and low levels of warmth. Above all else, these parents want obedience from and control of their children. It's a 'my way or the highway' kind of situation where rules are set with little or no explanation; simply a case of 'because I said so'. And if these rules are broken, children often face harsh and disproportionate punishments, with parents believing they are entirely reasonable. Talking back is a huge 'no-no' as is expressing an opinion or feelings, or communicating in any way that the parent deems inappropriate or a challenge to their authority. This kind of parenting creates a frightening atmosphere. These children often become adults who struggle with low self-esteem, anxiety, sadness or anger, making life feel like a struggle. They have difficulties with autonomy and making decisions for themselves because they weren't allowed to. Their history of emotional suppression makes it hard for them to express their feelings. And, because they weren't allowed to show their emotions, they never had the chance to learn, or be taught, how to regulate them. Forming healthy relationships can also be hard for these adults.

Permissive parenting – the indulgent approach

Permissive parenting has a high level of warmth but almost no boundaries; it's also known as indulgent parenting. Parents allow children as much freedom as they want. These parents can be almost obsessed with the child's desires, and the child, in turn, can also be obsessed with getting their way. People often refer to these children as spoiled or self-centred. Regardless of how the child behaves, parents rarely discipline them. Children raised this way might say, 'My parent is more like a friend,' and often the parent has the same view. Even though this kind of parenting can make a child feel loved and supported, the level of permissiveness can create serious problems down the line. These children can grow up to be adults who struggle with responsibility, accountability, authority and limit setting. They also struggle with respecting other people's boundaries. They can be impulsive and want things quickly because they're used to instant gratification. They often have a sense of entitlement, and when they don't get what they want, they can have intense emotional reactions. They often don't know how to deal with these emotions, because their parents gave in to their every whim, which left no opportunity to learn emotional regulation skills.

Uninvolved parenting – the neglectful approach

These parents are dismissive, unresponsive and uninvolved in their child's life. There's not just an absence of warmth; these parents can also be cold towards their children. In this type of parenting, there is a lack of boundaries and a failure to meet a child's most basic physical and emotional needs. Parents with this style provide minimal, if any, emotional support. They are uninterested in their child's life, thoughts, feelings or opinions. Children raised in these families experience the parent as emotionally and physically absent. I'm stating the obvious when I say that growing up like this really messes up adult life. These adults often end up feeling bad about themselves, like they're not worth anything; they have a tough time with relationships, struggle with trust and handling their emotions, and even just taking care of themselves. They also face an increased risk of mental health problems, substance abuse, personality difficulties, behavioural problems and employment issues.

It's heartbreaking to think that there are children out there going through this, and I'm sure it's tough to read about too.

Like many people, you might wonder how anyone could treat a child this way. When I worked with children and families in these situations, I was often asked this question. Many of these families ended up in court, with legal action being taken against them. The entire team wondered whether the harmful parenting came from mental health struggles, past trauma or intentional neglect. In my experience, it was a mixture, sometimes the result of a parent's unresolved personal struggles, and other times it was wilful neglect.

Exploring these different parenting styles isn't about placing blame, it's about holding compassion and acceptance for yourself as that small innocent child, and for the past you couldn't control. It's also about understanding where some of your challenges might come from and recognizing that you're not stuck because of how you were raised. I've seen it happen time and again, and it's one of the powerful aspects of being a clinical psychologist: people who've experienced problematic parenting learning to turn things around for themselves. And that's what this book is about: understanding, learning and doing things differently, so you can move forward in a better way.

Chapter 4: How People and Culture Shape You

Beyond your home environment, where attachment and parenting play a key role, the people you encounter in life also leave their mark. People can broaden your perspective, by showing you new ways of thinking and being which can then change how you are and how you see yourself. This can happen with friends, peers, colleagues or others – they can all strengthen your beliefs and also make you question them. Your interactions with people also influence your confidence, emotional intelligence and personal growth, shaping who you are and who you want to become. You might see characteristics in others you admire and want to embody, and equally, you might see things you dislike and think may never be part of you.

Sometimes we're aware of the things we pick up from other people but often it just happens without us even realizing. From childhood, we're shaped by the people we play with, learn from and grow up around, learning about sharing, fairness, conflict and connection. And that doesn't stop when we grow up, it continues all through life in the many friendships and relationships we have. When those relationships are healthy, they shape you in healthy ways. Healthy people can strengthen the foundations you already have from your home life. These relationships can also help you grow into new parts of yourself so you feel stronger and more sure of who you are. Through these people, you learn so much – how to communicate, how to deal with disagreements, how to say no when you need to, how to stick up for yourself, and how to live life in a way that's right for you and helps you thrive.

Culture also brings its influence, through shared values, traditions, beliefs, ways of thinking, interacting and behaving. All of that can mould who we become. Some cultures really champion the sense of being an individual, encouraging you to embrace your uniqueness. In contrast, others lean more towards the importance of everyone fitting in with shared belief systems. These cultural currents shape how you communicate with people, form relationships, define success, and so much more. When the messages you receive from your culture line up with your strengths and who you naturally are, it can feel like things just fit; they feel right. This helps you have a more solid sense of yourself and your purpose. Culture is like the soil we grow in; it's rich in history, has depth and meaning, and is a base from which you take root. For some people, their culture will provide lasting nourishment throughout their lives. But for others, as life changes, not every part of that soil will nourish them in the same way for ever. Sometimes, the expectations culture brings can make you feel as if you're stuck in a tight box, with its spoken and unspoken rules limiting who you are and how you want to live. This can create an inner tug-of-war between who you think you should be, who you really are or even who you want to become. On top of this, by being around other people, their cultures and their ideas, you might realize there are other things that feel like a better fit for you. But at the same time, these might clash with the cultural values you've grown up with or had instilled into you. If that's your experience, always remember it's okay to find your own balance. You don't have to abandon your roots, but you can absolutely choose which parts of your culture genuinely nourish you and are worth holding onto and which ones you might want to let go of. You can honour where you come from, respect your heritage and also embrace your uniqueness.

The way people treat you, their words, actions, energy, and the feelings they stir in you, can also shape who you are. The negatives you pick up from people can plant seeds of doubt, fear and insecurity. You're more susceptible to this during adolescence, when fitting in and being accepted feel like everything. If you're treated badly, a fear of rejection can take hold early in life, shaping how you relate to others because of what you start to believe about yourself in relation to them. If you've ever been ignored, criticized or excluded, you'll know how quickly it can make you second-guess your worth – and how that can lead you to react in all kinds of self-protective ways. People-pleasing often develops at this point, because approval becomes your currency. You might let people take advantage of you, because their acceptance becomes your source of validation. You might pull away completely, move into healthier relationships or retreat into isolation. When people affect you negatively, it can erode your ability to set boundaries. It can make it hard to say no or stand up for yourself. You learn to avoid conflict and suppress your feelings just to keep the peace. The problem is that when these patterns continue they leave you vulnerable to unhealthy relationships, where you get manipulated or treated badly. And the longer it goes on, the more it shapes what you think about yourself, and what you believe you deserve. When you believe you deserve less, you can easily end up stuck in repeated patterns of unhealthy relationships, unknowingly seeking out what feels familiar even if it hurts you, because it fits with what you believe. Sometimes people stay in these unhealthy dynamics for years, believing it's just how relationships are meant to feel. Often, it's because the slow slide into them makes it harder to recognize what healthy actually looks like, especially when it's not been your main experience.

Regardless of whether it's people or culture, the key is recognizing and understanding which influences have shaped you, and in what ways, so you know what serves you and what limits you. When you start to see things clearly, you can make choices that match who you want to be, and who you already are underneath everything else. It's worth asking yourself, who are the people in your life that really bring out the best in you? Who makes you feel more like yourself? And are there relationships that pull you away from that?

Chapter 5:
How Trauma Can Shape You

Trauma is an emotional response to something painful and overwhelming. Trauma is the invisible weight many of us carry, and it shapes us in ways we don't always fully understand or even recognize. Trauma of all kinds can weave its way into how we see ourselves, how we interact with others, and how we let people treat us. This is especially true for relational trauma, which is all about people. It's the kind of trauma where your sense of safety, trust or emotional wellbeing gets shaken by someone else. Since this book is all about you and how others affect you, shaping who you are in ways you don't want, like or can't break free from, my focus here will mainly be on relational trauma. There are lots of ways relational trauma can show up, and here are just some of the most common ones.

Bullying	Witnessing harm
Emotional abuse	Relationship breakdown
Verbal abuse	Betrayal
Toxic friendships	Humiliation
Toxic relationships	Physical harm
Childhood neglect	Loss

The trauma may have happened in the past, but its effects don't stay there. It quietly echoes in the present, influencing the choices you make and the patterns you find yourself in. And regardless of whether it happened years ago or more recently, whether it was big or small, it can still affect who you are today. It's not the size of the trauma that dictates how deeply it affects you. What feels traumatic to one person might not land the same way for someone else. That doesn't make it any less valid though. The impact of trauma depends on all kinds of things – your personality, your resilience, the support you had around you (or lack of it), and how your nervous system processes stress. It's about how distressing it was for you. And if someone else walked away from a similar experience seemingly unaffected, that doesn't mean yours isn't valid or didn't leave a mark.

Trauma can shape what you expect from others, how you show up and what you believe you deserve. Relational trauma can leave you feeling worthless, because it means you've been treated as if you didn't matter. It can set beliefs like 'I'm not good enough' or 'I'm not loveable' into your mind. And when you carry beliefs like these, you're always bracing yourself for problems with others. For instance, it might be a fear of rejection that pops up in small moments, like waiting for a reply that never comes or takes too long, or in bigger fears, like worrying that people will exclude you or sensing judgement when it's not there.

Boundaries can also be hard, because trauma itself is a violation of them, and it skews your understanding of where limits should lie. You might not even know that boundaries are a thing. Even when you do know about them, you might not know where to start with them. You might even wonder if you're allowed to have boundaries, or allowed to say no. You might also worry that if you set boundaries, people will react negatively to you, reinforcing a sense of fear and insecurity about having choice and control over yourself.

Trauma can also make it harder to be assertive. At the time of the trauma, staying quiet or passive might have felt like the safest way to avoid more harm, making passivity a kind of survival tool. But when this carries on over time, this passive response can become a habit, making it tough to assert yourself even in safe situations. People-pleasing can often be tied to past trauma in this way too. In the moment of trauma, pleasing others might again have been a way to stay safe or minimize harm, another survival instinct. It's that belief, 'If I do what they want, and please them, everything will be better.' But this can leave you constantly searching outside yourself for validation, instead of trusting that your worth is already there.

Trauma can also shape how you view conflict, often making it feel bigger and more threatening than it actually is. This makes sense, because conflict can stir up the same feelings of vulnerability and helplessness you might have had during the trauma. Because of this, you might believe that even small disagreements have the potential to spiral into something overwhelming or dangerous, with confrontation causing you instant anxiety. Sometimes, people can have the opposite reaction, where they might overcompensate, reacting aggressively at the first sign of conflict almost as a defensive or protective mechanism to prevent themselves from being mistreated.

When you have difficulties with boundaries, assertiveness, people-pleasing and dealing with conflict, it can also mean you're more likely to tolerate toxic behaviour from others. Firstly, because you don't know how to address it. Secondly, you might allow it because it feels familiar. Thirdly, you don't believe that you deserve any better. You might also find yourself stuck in old patterns of letting toxic behaviour slide, out of fear of being hurt again.

When you carry beliefs like you're not good enough, it's also very easy to slip into making negative comparisons with others. Even though comparison is something we all do, trauma can twist it into something much more harsh and painful, with you measuring yourself against other people to try and figure out how worthy you are and what you're lacking.

Trauma can pull you away from yourself, and away from how you want to be. It can also make it harder to know what's going on inside you. What you're feeling and why you're feeling it, and why you react the way you do. That's because, at the time of the trauma, your system was overwhelmed, and there wasn't space to sit with what was happening, it was about surviving. For a lot of people, it remains about surviving long after the threat is gone. So those patterns stick around, even when they no longer serve you. It's easy to end up on autopilot with them, going through life in ways that don't really feel like you, simply because you haven't had the chance or space to pause, notice and choose differently. As we wrap up this chapter and move into Part 2, that's exactly what we'll focus on: finding your way back to yourself. We'll explore your personal values and how you can use them to rebuild a sense of self that feels authentic, the self that's already there beneath all the old patterns, and that isn't defined by fear or past hurts. This gives you something solid to stand on, even when old habits or reactions try to pull you off course. It's what helps you reclaim the power these experiences may have taken from you. Later, in Part 10, we'll look more closely at moving past relational wounds. Ultimately, it's all about learning to let go of what holds you back and living more fully as the person you really are.

Things to hold onto . . .

How you are is shaped by so many things, the genetics and temperament you're born with, your personality, your attachment style, the parenting you've received, how others and culture influence you, and also how trauma might have affected you.

All of these things affect how you think, feel, act and relate to others.

Whether it's an insecure attachment style, trauma or habits, none of it is completely set in stone. As human beings, we have the potential for growth, transformation and change at any point in our lives.

Change can mean moving from an insecure attachment style to an earned-secure one that you've worked hard to achieve for yourself through your own effort.

Part Two

Find Yourself Through Your Values

'Don't copy, it's not nice.' It's what we're told as kids, yet we all do it at some point. Why? Because we don't always know how else to be. Without a strong sense of our own identity or values, other people become our map. But trying to do what they do, trying to be who they are never feels quite right, does it? It can feel disconnected, like you're shaping yourself around someone else's mould, hoping it will fit you too. But it's hard work because it's not truly you. If only it were easy to know who you are and how you want to be, without needing to look to someone else for that sense of direction. I want to tell you about Becky, someone who felt exactly like this. 'I don't know how to be who I am, or what that even is,' Becky said, staring into the distance. 'I feel like I've been a nobody for years, just copying what everyone else does. I dress like them, I walk, talk and act like them, I probably think like them. I hang out with people I don't really like, doing pointless things. I'm just so lost and don't know who I'm supposed to be. So, I just latch onto others and base my ideas of how I should be on how they are. I even copy the phrases they say. I've always latched onto other people, copying them – friends, family, people online, people at school, college, then work. I feel like I imitate their personality. Pretty much everything about me is because of trying to be like someone else. Growing up, I did what my parents wanted me to do, being what they said I should be like. Then I tried to fit into what others were like because I didn't know how else to be. I wish I had a solid idea of myself, I don't want to be an NPC.'

An NPC is a non-playable character in a video game. They're the people in the background, just passing by, walking around, the extras. They're the fillers, they don't have a part in the main narrative. NPCs don't do anything independently. They do the thing they've been told to do – well, programmed to do. No matter how many buttons you press on the controller, NPCs don't break from their loop, they just carry on following someone else's game plan, and they don't have one of their own. Becky used the example of NPCs because she felt like she'd been following someone else's script. She'd been going through the motions of life, mimicking others, without truly 'living' or defining her own path. Just like NPCs are stuck in the same loop, Becky felt stuck in a loop of not being herself, or knowing how to be herself, because she didn't know what that even was.

Do you relate to Becky's experience? When we're unsure of ourselves, it's so easy to lose ourselves to the influence of others, and it often can happen without us even realizing it. But why is this? It's often because we don't have an anchor, something solid that keeps us grounded to who we really are, because we don't know what that is. That insecurity makes it feel so much easier and safer to just blend in, doing what others do, and thinking how they think. It's the simpler option, and way easier than trying to figure out what you want or how you really want to be. Not to mention how tough it can feel to go against the grain and be different. When we try to do something that feels outside the norm, it can feel like we're stepping into the spotlight. Like people might notice us, and that can be pretty scary. The good news is, you don't have to stay stuck in that cycle of just following what others are doing, thinking or feeling. You can be yourself. In this part, I'm going to show you how to find the anchor that grounds you in who you truly want to be, who you really are based on your values, and how you can start living that way. When you do this, life can feel more authentic and more *you*. The idea of what makes a good life – and a life that feels like yours – has been around for centuries, with ancient philosophers being the first to bring attention to it. Over time, sociology and psychology began to understand how values shape both our behaviours and our differences. Humanistic psychology took this further, highlighting the importance of personal meaning, growth and an inner compass, bringing values even more to the forefront. As psychological theories continued to develop, we saw more practical frameworks for understanding how values can be extremely useful drivers of our behaviour and have a big influence on our well-being. The concept of values is well researched; by the mid to late twentieth century, the understanding of values in psychology evolved in such meaningful ways that it is now part of many psychological therapies, such as Acceptance and Commitment Therapy (ACT).[7]

Chapter 1:
What Are Values?

Imagine you're walking down the street, all by yourself, when you spot a wallet on the ground, stuffed with money. It could be your lucky day. The temptation to keep it flashes through your mind for a second. You could buy a few things, treat yourself. But then, if honesty is something that really matters to you, that feeling won't last long. Deep down, you know it just wouldn't feel right to keep it. Your core value of honesty gently but firmly nudges you and, suddenly, that tempting idea shifts into something that feels distinctly off. So, you return it. And honestly? It feels pretty good because you acted in a way that honours what matters most to you. And this is the inherent power of having values!

I want to make a distinction between values and goals, because people often get them mixed up. Even though both impact the direction your life takes and what your life feels like, they are different. Values are about how you walk through life, they're your compass that gets you back on track, no matter what path you take. Whereas goals are more like the milestones you hit while you're moving in the direction of your values. Picture it as a journey, your goals are the destinations or places along the way, like a beach, a mountain or a museum, that you can check off once you've been there. Values, on the other hand, are about the kind of traveller you want to be while you're on that journey. They influence your experience of the journey itself, no matter where you end up or how many places you get to visit or check off. For example, if fun is one of your values, you'll find situations along the way that make the journey enjoyable. Or if beauty is one of your values you'll keep your eyes open to all the beautiful things on your journey, like the scenery, nature and animals. Even if the road gets bumpy, you can still hold onto your values of fun and beauty – a sunset is still beautiful, even if the ground beneath you is uneven.

So, to recap, values are your sense of direction, they shape how you live, who you are in the present and in the future. Goals are specific things you want to achieve. Goals can be completed, but values can't, they persist throughout your life. Values come from within you, but goals are external to you. Values focus on how you show up and experience every moment, but goals are about reaching specific moments in the future.

Chapter 2:
Why Values Matter So Much

For a long time studies have shown how much our values matter for how we think and feel, and for feeling okay in ourselves.[8] They act as guiding principles that give life purpose, meaning and direction, that's why they're often part of therapy. They play a powerful role in helping you connect with what truly matters. They shape the choices you make and strengthen your sense of who you are. And when you're living in line with your values, life just feels more meaningful. Because you're not just reacting to things on autopilot – you're choosing them. Your values help you answer the big question that comes up time and again – and that question is: what really matters? And once you know that, it changes the way you move through life. Even the hard stuff starts to feel a little more purposeful, because it's connected to something deeper. Circumstances will always change, that's life. But your values are the anchor you can come back to. They keep you steady. They give you a way to stay connected to yourself, even when everything around you feels uncertain. Having your sense of self grounded in your values is like having a really strong base that can help you deal with whatever life throws your way. This isn't about trying to be perfect, because nobody is. It's about getting in touch with the real you, the core of who you already are, and showing up in the world and with people in a way that feels right.

Living according to your values reduces the inner conflict

that can come from doing things that don't align with who you really are. It also stops you from falling into the trap of doing things just to meet other people's expectations, instead of meeting your own expectations of yourself. Not only does this help you connect with who you really are, it can also improve your mental health. Research has found that living by your values can protect against depression and anxiety.[9] Thinking about what matters most to you can also be a great way to manage stress; the research shows that people who affirmed their values had lower levels of cortisol, a stress hormone that is released by your body when you're feeling under pressure, compared to those who didn't.

But it's not just about reducing stress, living this way also builds a deeper sense of self-trust and agency. Values are like little reminders that no matter what's going on around you, you still get to choose how you're going to respond – and the kind of person you want to be in that moment. And that's powerful. That sense of agency strengthens your relationship with yourself, helps you feel more resilient, and builds real confidence from the inside out. Research has found that people who prioritize living in line with their values tend to be more resilient when life gets tough.[10] It shows how coming back to what really matters to you can strengthen your ability to cope, even in the face of stress or adversity. Research also shows that the more people live in line with their values, the better they tend to feel, with higher well-being and lower levels of stress and struggle.[11] The study also found that consistency matters. Fluctuating too often between living in line with your values and acting against them had the opposite effect, and was linked to lower well-being and more distress over time. You can see why it's worth taking the time to get clear on your values, and have something solid to come back to, especially when life gets tough.

Chapter 3:
How to Define Your Values

Let's get to the heart of it, and work step by step to uncover the values that sit at the core of who you are. Not the version of you others have expected. Not the shape you've bent into to be accepted, approved of or understood. This is about coming back to what feels right, not just on the surface but deep inside you. As you go through this process, try to gently set aside the outside noise. The subtle pressures, the narratives you've carried around about who you should be. And instead, listen to the voice inside you that already knows who you are and what really matters to you.

When you feel yourself drawn to a certain value ask yourself: 'Am I choosing this because it feels true to me, in my gut and in my heart? Or because it feels like what someone else would want for me?' There's no shame in either answer, just a gentle opportunity to notice. And if the pull is coming from outside of you, take a breath and ask yourself: 'Will it feel good, solid and honest to stand by this value? Will my life feel meaningful if I live by it? And, will I feel like I am living for myself?'

Values aren't just about one part of your life. They show up everywhere – in how you are with your family, friends, in your relationships, in your work and in how you treat yourself when nobody else is looking. So, as you define your values, think broadly about all these areas. You might notice certain values showing up again and again, regardless of the life context. That's not random – it's a sign. They're speaking to something true in you, so pay attention to them.

Here are the different life areas to keep in mind:

Health and well-being	Family
Education / Career	Friends
Leisure	Community
Personal growth	Relationships
Religion or spirituality	Environment

Step 1: Create three headings in a journal. Do this on a piece of paper or in a digital notebook:

'Most Important to Me'
'Somewhat Important to Me'
'Not Important to Me'

Step 2: Discover Your Core Values. Now, go through the list of values in the boxes on pp. 43–4 and sort them by placing each under one of the three headings you've created. If you think of other values that aren't on my list, then feel free to include them as well. Take a moment to read through your list of 'Most Important to Me' values and reflect on each one by asking yourself these questions:

- Does this value reflect qualities that are important to me?

- Is this value truly me?

- Is this value a trait I admire?
- Would having this value make me proud?
- Is this a value I want to stand for?
- Does this value represent a non-negotiable quality?
- Is this value something I want to be remembered for?
- How do I want to be in difficult situations?
- If no one was watching, what would I still choose to do?
- How do I want to treat others and myself, and what do I expect to be treated like in return?

The Values Table

Acceptance	Empathy
Adaptability	Excitement
Adventure	Fairness
Assertiveness	Fitness
Beauty	Flexibility
Caring	Forgiveness
Challenge	Freedom
Collaboration	Friendliness
Compassion	Fun
Confidence	Generosity
Connection	Gratitude
Contribution	Hard-working
Courage	Harmony
Creativity	Health
Determination	Honesty

Humility	Safety
Humour	Self-awareness
Independence	Self-control
Intimacy	Self-development
Kindness	Self-discipline
Love	Self-expression
Organization	Self-respect
Patience	Self-love
Pleasure	Social connection
Resilience	Solitude
Respect	Stability
Responsibility	Trust

Step 3: Rank and Identify Your Core Values. Now take the values that you've listed under 'Most Important to Me' and set the lists under the other two headings aside. Review your list of Most Important values and arrange them in order of importance, from most important to you to least important. After that, focus on your top ten values and rank them by numbering them 1 to 10. It's perfectly fine if you have fewer than ten values. The goal is to clearly identify your most important values: your number one, your top three and your top five. If you have more than ten values on this list, this ranking process will help you narrow them down by letting go of those that fall outside your top ten.

Now that you have your top values, keep a special note of them; you can write them in the box over the page, in your journal or in your digital notes.

My Core Values

1
2
3
4
5
6
7
8
9
10

Chapter 4:
How to Live by Your Values

Now that you have a list of your values let's take a look at how your everyday life matches up with them. Think of your values as your framework to live by. This process is about checking in to see if you're actually following that set of rules in your day-to-day life. And the reason we want to do this is to spot any big differences between how you want to be living, and how you're actually living right now. If there are any big gaps, those are your clues. They show you where to make changes that could help life feel richer and more meaningful.

For example, if one of your values is self-respect, and you notice that you let people pressure you, people-please, or are harsh on yourself in your own head, these are signs that your actions aren't lining up with the value. To live by self-respect, you have to learn how to say no, be kinder to yourself, understand what your needs are – and meet them. We'll talk more about how you do all of that later in the book.

How aligned are you with your values?

Take a moment to rank your values based on how aligned you feel you are with each one right now. Use a scale from 0 to 10, where 10 means you're fully living in line with that value, and

0 means you're not living by it at all. There's a table below to jot it all down; if you have fewer than ten values, that's totally fine, just rate the ones you have.

Value	Alignment (0–10)
1	
2	
3	
4	
5	
6	
7	
8	
9	
10	

When you've done that, take a moment to reflect on your rankings. Does anything surprise you? Which values feel like they're already part of your life, and which ones need more of your attention? This reflection isn't just for awareness, it's your guide. Your lower-scoring values will show you exactly where you need to focus more of your energy. The next step is about turning those insights into meaningful, realistic actions, keeping the values that feel most out of alignment in mind as you move forward.

Taking action that reflects your values

Now that you've got a clearer picture of how aligned you are with your values, it's time to turn that insight into action. You won't be able to work on everything all at once; this is about small, steady steps that help you move closer to the kind of life you want, and the kind of person you want to be. For example, if you value being assertive but feel far from it right now, maybe because you haven't had the tools or practice yet, expecting to suddenly become assertive overnight isn't realistic. This part is about breaking that down into doable steps. (And if assertiveness is one of your values, you'll find a whole section on it in Part 5.)

Take your list of important values, and for each one, write down a few actions you can take to move closer to it, and live more in line with it. The first step might simply be reflecting on why it's been hard to live by that value, or thinking about what needs to shift. Even that counts as action. When you're setting an action for each value, ask yourself how much that action reflects the value, to make sure that it's meaningful. To show you how this works, here's an example using Sam's values and the actions he's chosen to move closer to each one.

Sam's Values and Corresponding Actions

Value	Action
Harmony	Be calm and patient during disagreements, there's no urgency to speak. I can wait for the other person to finish first. Accept that other people will feel differently to me. Manage conflict better.

Gratitude	Note down one thing I'm grateful for every day. Focus on the present moment instead of thinking about what's next. Share my appreciation more with people around me.
Stability	Keep a consistent routine, especially during the week, so I can manage everything more easily. Avoid unhealthy dynamics with others. Avoid impulsive decisions; revisit any that come up after 3 days to get clarity.
Courage	Speak up even when it feels uncomfortable. Try new things that push me out of my comfort zone. Take responsibility for my mistakes and learn from them. Set and pursue goals that seem intimidating.
Social connection	Make time to see my friends, even if it feels like a lot of effort. Regularly get in touch with people I am close to and maintain contact through a weekly message. Arrange a monthly social event with family. Be open to meeting new people by trying a new hobby.
Independence	Be comfortable making my own decisions. Go to places I usually visit with others, but by myself. Try something new.
Assertiveness	Learn how to express my needs and feelings openly and respectfully. Practise saying no and get better at it. Say no to people-pleasing. Look for opportunities to practise assertiveness in small, easy everyday situations.

Self-compassion	Speak kindly to myself, just as I would to a friend. Accept that I am human and will make mistakes. Don't criticize myself or be harsh on myself when things go wrong. Say no to things so I can take time to rest and recharge when life is busy. Set boundaries with people to protect my mental health.
Self-respect	Set clear boundaries with people who make me uncomfortable. Prioritize my needs and well-being, even if it means saying no. Choose relationships with people who treat me with respect and distance myself from those that don't. Speak positively about myself instead of constantly criticizing myself.
Health	Exercise for at least 30 minutes a few times a week, such as by walking home. Set boundaries to get off screens by 9 p.m. so I can get 7–8 hours of sleep. Plan meals and shopping so I eat a balanced diet with fruits, vegetables and whole foods.

Sam's example shows you his general overarching goals, all of which can be broken down even further. The goals you set in relation to your values can be short-term, long-term or in-the-moment. What they should all have in common is that they make the bigger goals feel more achievable and keep you moving in the direction of your values. If any of this feels like too much, remember you can start small. Just pick one or two simple actions for each value to start with, then build on them over time until they become a part of your everyday life.

Every step you take towards your values is progress, so no matter how you start, it matters. Change often begins with the smallest actions and, sometimes, setbacks are part of the process too. Living by your values isn't about perfect progress, there will be ups and downs, moments when you don't quite line up with your values. When that happens, don't beat yourself up. Just remember you're human. Show yourself some kindness, think about what made things tough and figure out what might help you stay on track next time. Then, just keep going.

It's good practice to check in on your values every now and then because, as you go through different stages in life, your priorities might shift. Life events can change the way you see things, a new relationship, becoming a parent, moving to another place, facing a health issue or a loss and sometimes just getting older can make you reconsider your values. So it helps to check in on them every so often, especially after something big happens, to make sure they still line up with what really matters to you.

Chapter 5:
Staying on Track

Now that you've got your values in place and you're starting to see how your actions can line up with them, let's think about staying connected to them. It's easy for values to fade into the background when life gets busy or distractions start pulling you off course. Here are some simple, easy ways to stay connected to them:

- Write your values down and keep them somewhere you'll see them often on paper or digitally. If they're on your phone or computer, you can also set a little reminder to have them pop up during the day.
- Read them once a day (this can be especially helpful when you're just getting started) or in those moments when everything feels uncertain, and you need something solid to come back to.
- As you go through your day, keep an eye out for opportunities to act on your values.
- When you're making a decision, big or small, pause and check in with your values. Ask yourself which choice feels most in line with them – and let that guide you.
- In tough times when everything else feels uncertain and difficult, use your values to guide how you want to move through it.

- At the start of the day, you can ask yourself: 'What's one thing I can do today that moves me towards one of my values?' Name the value and name the action.

- At the end of the day, check back in with yourself: 'What did I do today that aligned with one of my values?'

- You can also set an intention for the day. Something like: 'Today I want to live out the value of kindness, and I'll do that by calling my friend just to check in.'

- Make a vision board, as a visual reminder of what matters most to you. You can go old-school with paper and pins, or make a digital version – whatever you prefer. Add your core values, with images, quotes or symbols that capture the actions or feelings tied to them.

- Use visualization. Let your mind wander to a future version of yourself living by any one of your values. Picture a clear moment from that life. What are you doing? How are you treating yourself and others? What's one thing you feel really proud of? This glimpse into your future can show you how your choices today matter. It's like looking at the destination on your map – a reminder of where you're headed and what is really important.

Things to hold onto . . .

You can live more in line with who you truly are by figuring out what really matters to you – these are your values.

Values are like a framework, a compass, a quiet guide. They're the principles you choose that give your life direction and meaning. When you follow them, you stay connected to what feels right for you. They're a powerful tool – helping you build a stronger sense of who you are and how you want to live.

Living by your values eases the inner conflict that comes from doing things that don't really sit right with who you are. It also stops you spending your life doing things just to meet other people's expectations, rather than your own.

When you know what your values are, you can keep choosing, moment by moment, to live in line with them. And in difficult times you can come back to them, they're your steady ground, so that even when things feel uncertain, you're still acting from a place that's true to you.

Part Three

Freedom from the Fear of Rejection

Leo had a fear of rejection that went all the way back to childhood. He grew up with parents who were emotionally distant – love and approval weren't freely given, and criticism came far more easily than affection. Over time, he started to believe that if his own parents couldn't accept him, why would anyone else? That belief settled in deep, and Leo developed a fear of being rejected again. At university Leo found a good mixed group of friends, they got on so well, and had a lot of fun together. He was single, and pretty avoidant when it came to forming close emotional connections. It wasn't that he didn't want love, he did, but avoiding it felt safer than risking feeling rejected. At times, he even questioned whether his friends genuinely liked him, or if they were just being polite.

Leo developed a crush on one of the girls in the group, let's call her Carmen. She was warm, kind and funny. Because he had a deep craving for acceptance from others, he convinced himself there was something special between them – even though, from the outside, it seemed like Carmen was just being friendly in the same way she was with everyone. Leo didn't say anything about how he felt to her for a long time. His past rejection wounds made him hold back. He needed a guarantee – a clear sign – before he'd risk putting himself out there. So instead, he clung to hope. He held onto the version of the story he wanted to be true, rather than facing reality.

Eventually, he did tell Carmen how he felt. He brought flowers and a small gift, wanting the moment to be meaningful. She let him down gently, kindly, but clearly – Carmen didn't feel the same way. She just saw Leo as a friend. And of course, she was completely within her rights to feel that, it's not cruel or cold if someone doesn't feel the way you want them to. You can't make someone, or expect them to, feel something they don't, this isn't in your control. But Leo was devastated, not only because Carmen didn't return his feelings, but because it hit something deeper. In his mind, it confirmed what he feared all along – that he wasn't enough. That maybe his parents were right about him after all. This is the trap so many people fall into, tying their sense of worth to someone else's response. The problem is, someone else's feelings are shaped by their own experiences, their timing, what they're ready for – not by your value as a person. When you base your worth on that, you hand it over to someone who was never meant to be responsible for it.

The rejection stung, and it shook Leo's sense of worth even more. Leo had avoided clarity because of fear, and the longer he'd waited, the more attached he'd got to the idea of him and Carmen – not as she was, but the version he'd built in his mind. And as that story grew, so did the fear of it falling apart. So when the rejection finally came, it hit hard. One thing I told Leo, and something that still holds true now, is this: someone else's feelings don't define your worth. Rejection is painful, of course it is – but it's not personal in the way you think it is. We all want to be seen, accepted and loved. But when your value gets tied to a particular person's approval, especially someone who never signed up to hold that responsibility, it's a set-up for heartbreak.

Leo fell into a kind of limerence after this – that all-consuming longing for someone who doesn't feel the same way. (We'll talk more about limerance in Part 10.) The truth is, he was already in it even before he told Carmen how he felt. It took time but eventually he moved through the limerance. Leo had to learn how to come back to himself, to figure out what actually mattered to him, what kind of life he wanted, and who he wanted to be, with or without someone else beside him. He had to learn to find his worth from within, not in whether someone else returned his feelings. Some people are for you, and some people aren't – and that's not a reflection of your value, it's just part of life. And, it's a lesson we all have to learn.

Fear of rejection isn't just about romantic situations – it can show up with friends, family, in your education, your career, even in the way you treat yourself, and how you allow others to treat you. It's not just about avoiding a 'no' from people – it's about protecting the parts of you that once felt rejected, unseen, criticized and not good enough. Those early experiences shape how you show up now, how much of yourself you reveal, whether you speak up or stay quiet, whether you take risks or hold back from the things you want – because of the fear that rejection might be waiting.

And when that fear's in the driver's seat, it can make you play small, stay silent and shrink to stay safe. In this part of the book, we'll explore what fear of rejection really is, where it comes from, how it shows up – and most importantly, how you can stop it from running your life.

Chapter 1:
What Is Fear of Rejection?

Rejection really is a normal part of life, and it's something you, I and everyone else have experienced and survived before – and we will all survive it again. Rejection is a universal experience; you can ask anyone you know, and they will have a story to share about being rejected or fearing rejection. It's so common. And knowing that it happens to everyone can make you feel a little less alone.

The fear of rejection isn't just about someone saying no to you. It can also show up as the fear of not being liked – even if that's based on just your assumption. Maybe someone does act distant, and you think it means they don't like you – even though there could be so many other reasons for them acting that way that might have nothing to do with you. Or maybe they actually don't like you, just as you don't click with everyone either. You may fear not fitting in, being judged or being treated in ways that make you feel like you don't matter. It can show up in many contexts and relationships, in friendships, romantic situations, family dynamics, at work, even in being excluded or ignored in casual everyday encounters. Romantic relationships and dating can stir up so many fears of rejection. There's the worry about not being wanted, the sting of someone saying no, or the ache that comes with feeling that you're just not attractive to them. It can feel personal, even when it's not – and it hurts, because deep down, we all want to feel seen and valued.

It might be about being excluded when others make plans without you or when you're the only one reaching out. Why a friend doesn't get back to you about meeting up, or cancels last minute. Family life can also stir up the fear of rejection. You might feel like you have to shape yourself into a version of who they want you to be, in order to feel accepted. And to avoid the sting of rejection, you might start doing things that don't feel true to you, like saying yes when you want to say no, or hiding parts of yourself just to keep the peace, or to feel like you belong. At work, the fear of rejection might show up in a job interview, a performance review or just not being recognized for what you bring to the table. Meeting new people can also trigger feelings of inadequacy. Even in casual, everyday encounters, fear of rejection shows up. It might be a situation where you say something only to feel ignored, as if you're invisible while everyone else seems seen. Or you might struggle with making phone calls, replying to emails or sending messages, because you dread the possibility of feeling rejected through a negative or delayed response.

The fear of being rejected isn't only face-to-face any more. In this digital age, we're also vulnerable to rejection – or the perception of it – online. It's easy to find things that seem to confirm those fears – like seeing what others are doing without you and wondering, 'Why wasn't I included?' It might sound insignificant, but not getting a response to a message, being left on read, or seeing someone view your story but not like or reply can trigger that familiar ache. And it hits even harder when it's from someone you see as a friend, a family member or someone you have a connection with and care about. You might spiral into questions like: Did I say something wrong? They liked someone else's post? Am I not interesting enough? Do they not like me any more? Social media can turn connection into comparison fast – and we'll get into how to deal with that in Part 8. Of course, there are algorithms and many other factors at play – but in moments that trigger rejection fears, your brain isn't thinking logically. It's reacting emotionally. And that feeling of being ignored or unseen can land hard, tapping straight into those deeper fears of not being accepted or valued.

The fear of rejection isn't just about the act itself – it's the expectation that it will happen because it has before. People who struggle with this fear often avoid situations where rejection might occur. It's natural to want to protect yourself from that pain, but when you keep doing that it makes you more sensitive to the pain. What you really need is the opposite, to build resilience, so you can handle something that's not only common but an inevitable part of life.

Rejection doesn't just feel uncomfortable. Research shows that the brain treats rejection almost like physical pain.[12] It's not just something that happens in your head, your body actually reacts to it physically too. Some people are more sensitive to rejection – they feel it more deeply, and that makes it harder to manage the emotions it brings up. That sensitivity often comes from earlier wounds – moments when they felt rejected, criticized or not enough. And because the brain stores those moments as threats to belonging, and belonging is wired into us as a survival need, the fear gets amplified. When that sensitivity is high, rejection lingers. It can shake your confidence, make you doubt yourself more deeply and trigger a stronger emotional reaction. Rejection is painful, and the hurt you feel is a natural response. People don't feel joyful about being rejected. Feeling pain isn't a sign of weakness, it's a sign that you're human. It does not mean there's something wrong with you. But it may mean you need to find ways to manage that pain.

Another reason rejection can feel so intense is because of the patterns your brain builds from repeated experiences of it. When you've been rejected over and over, your brain starts to expect it. It can form neural pathways that anticipate rejection before it even happens, which can shape how you act – sometimes in ways that reinforce the very fear you're trying to avoid.

As you can see, a fear of rejection can ripple through your life. It can make you pull back before anyone else has a chance to say no. This might feel like protection, but really it's like closing the door on yourself before anyone else can. And when that happens, you turn away from experiences that might have brought joy, growth or connection. You might also hold back your opinions, or feelings, or try to keep the peace at all costs – anything to avoid being seen as too much.

Fear of rejection can make you live small to stay safe. Shrinking yourself, staying quiet, convincing yourself your needs don't matter. The irony is that you fear rejection because something has already made you feel bad about yourself. Then you act in ways dictated by that fear by hiding parts of yourself. In doing so, you end up proving to yourself that you are not enough, and that keeps you trapped in the very place you were trying to escape.

For some people, fear of rejection shows up as people-pleasing. Where you're living more for other people's comfort instead of your own. If you're a people-pleaser you'll know all too well how it can leave you feeling burnt out, resentful, and disconnected from what you really want and need. Fear of rejection can even keep you stuck in relationships or environments that harm you. In these scenarios the fear tells you it's safer to stay than to leave, even when you want to, because it's better than facing rejection somewhere else.

Fear of rejection might feel fixed; the good news is it isn't. With intention and repetition, you can change how you respond. You can lower the emotional weight of old rejections and start to rewire fear pathways – slowly building more grounded, less fearful responses. You can also build emotional skills that help you cope with the difficult feelings this fear brings up, so it doesn't define you or hold as much power over your choices.

Chapter 2: What Causes Fear of Rejection?

I'm sure you've wondered, why does rejection bother me so much? There are so many reasons that rejection hits hard. Starting with temperament and personality: if you're naturally sensitive or deeply attuned to other people's moods, you might be more reactive to negative social cues – and more likely to pick up on (or even look for) signs that someone is pulling away, even when nothing's been said outright.

Attachment styles play a part too. The way your caregivers responded to you growing up shapes what you expect from others later in life. If your early experiences were marked with emotional distance, criticism or unpredictability, it's natural to be more sensitive to rejection later on.

For some people, being excluded, bullied or humiliated early on is where the fear of rejection begins. Those moments can leave deep marks, and it makes sense to carry that fear of being judged or left out into the future.

Then there are the cultural and social messages. We live in a world that puts so much emphasis on being accepted, chosen, liked, approved of – even admired. There's not a lot of space for rejection to be seen as just a normal part of being human. Rejection is often framed as failure, which just piles on the pressure and the fear, making it feel like something you have to avoid at all costs.

Fear of rejection can also come from a single defining experience, something that happened to you, and the meaning you took from it left you questioning yourself. Maybe it was small, maybe it was big, but it left an imprint. That meaning often translates into thoughts like: I'm not wanted, I'm not good enough, I don't belong, I'll be rejected. And over time, those thoughts can shape how you move through life, becoming a filter that colours how you see everything, keeping the fear alive.

Chapter 3: Break Free from the Fear of Rejection

In this section, I'm going to walk you through seven actionable tools that can help you free yourself from the fear of rejection. We'll start with acceptance, how you can learn to sit with the fear, and then I'll show you how to process the emotions that surface when the fear of rejection shows up. We'll look at the thoughts that show up in these moments, and how you can see them in a more balanced light. We'll also look into how you can stop self-rejecting and lean into self-compassion instead. We'll talk about how you can find comfort in the connections you do have and, if those connections aren't there yet, we'll talk about how you can start building them in ways that feel doable. I'll show you how to move on from the impact of actual rejection, and we'll wrap up by looking at how your values can help you.

1. Acceptance

Acceptance is about being willing to acknowledge that rejection is something that can happen, and sometimes will happen. Acceptance is also about allowing the thoughts and feelings that come with it to show up, without trying to block them out, judge them or silence them. Acceptance means saying yes to the reality of your fear, knowing that it's valid, it's temporary and it doesn't define you. It's less about fixing your fear, and more about making space for it. And that's where the real shift begins – not by pushing the fear away, but by learning how to stay with yourself, even when it shows up.

Acceptance is about making space for the reality of having been rejected, just like everyone else. It's about recognizing that rejection isn't a personal flaw or some rare shameful failure, it's a normal part of being human, everyone faces it. And as painful as it can feel in the moment, that pain isn't permanent, it passes. Acceptance also means noticing that past experiences can leave traces or patterns that show up now and shape how you see things. Acceptance means opening yourself up to all of this, without the need to fight it, fix it or push it away. That doesn't mean you have to like rejection, no one does, it just means you're willing to let the experience be there, so you can move through it instead of staying stuck. From there, you can begin to build resilience, which is exactly what the skills in this section are about.

Acceptance also means making room for the thoughts that come with rejection fears, like 'I'm not good enough', without judgement. Not because they're true, but because they're there. You're not agreeing with them, and you're not arguing with them either, you're simply noticing that they're part of your experience at that moment. Judging a thought can make it feel heavier than it really is, as if it must be true. Acceptance is different, there's no judgement in it. You're letting the thought show up without needing to label it as good or bad, right or wrong. Just seeing it for what it is – your mind's natural response to a painful moment. Acceptance also means dropping the fight, that urge to push your experience away, to wish the situation was different or to scramble for a way to make all the discomfort disappear.

I know that acceptance can sometimes sound a bit abstract or vague, even a little fluffy. Many people I work with prefer something more concrete, something they can actually put into practice. If that's you, and simply telling yourself to 'accept it' feels too mental or passive, here's something more tangible you can try. You can practise acceptance by naming what's here and what's happening. That might mean saying it out loud or writing it down, whichever feels more helpful or grounding for you. You can do this whether it's a clear rejection, something that felt like rejection (even if you're not totally sure) or a fear that rejection might happen – just acknowledge it, in your own words. Here's what that might sound like:

'Yes, I have a fear of rejection.'

'Yes, I've been (or felt) rejected. I didn't get that job. That friend didn't want to meet up. That person didn't want a second date.'

'I accept that I sometimes avoid situations because I'm scared of being rejected.'

'I accept that some of my rejection fears today come from that experience I had back then.'

'I'm willing to accept my fears, to open up to them, even though I don't like them, because facing them is how I can begin to work through them.'

2. Process your feelings

Fear of rejection, and rejection itself, can bring up a lot of emotions: feelings of inadequacy, loneliness, sadness, anger. It might even be grief, especially if the person or opportunity mattered to you, or if the thought of what could have been meant a lot. Whatever shows up, let it. You're allowed to feel whatever you feel. Feeling it is how you start to process it. When you give your emotions room to be felt, they move. If you suppress or avoid them, they can become more intense and harder to handle. They can also eventually find a way to surface, either in your mind or body. When you process your feelings, it allows your mind to release them and move forward. This is because emotions have a natural life cycle that you can just flow through; once it's run its course, you can move past it. Processing your feelings this way also helps build your resilience, which makes it easier to handle tough emotions down the line.

So how do you actually process your feelings? You can use my 'Feel Your Feelings' method, which consists of the 5 Cs: Capture, Connect, Curiosity, Calm and Choose – you'll see it again later in the book. It's a straightforward five-step process that helps you navigate your emotions, no matter where they come from. It's a way for you to feel your emotions fully without getting stuck in them, you're letting them flow through you so you can find your balance and feel calm again.

Feel your feelings with the 5 Cs

1. **Capture:** When you feel rejected or afraid of rejection, notice the emotions that arise in you. Name them verbally, say, 'I am feeling . . .' or write them down.
2. **Connect:** Connect with these emotions by tuning into your body. Where do you feel them? What does that part of your body feel like? Maybe your stomach feels hollow, your heart races, or there's a lump in your throat.
3. **Curiosity:** Be curious about the thoughts that come with these feelings and just notice what they're telling

you. Maybe it's that no one will ever like you, or that you'll never succeed. You don't need to argue, react or try to make them go away – just observe them. Thoughts are simply thoughts, they're not facts.

4. **Calm:** What would soothe and calm the pain caused by these emotions? What does that hurt part of you need right now? What can you say or do that would be a compassionate response to these emotions? Say and do the things for yourself that bring you that comfort and calm.

5. **Choose:** Think about how you reacted to the situation that caused these feelings. Did you isolate yourself or tell yourself negative things? Instead of just sitting in the pain and letting it grow, think about an action you can take that helps you and aligns with your values, even while you're feeling this way. By choosing to take meaningful action despite the discomfort, you're showing yourself that you can still keep moving towards what matters most, regardless of the pain.

3. Deal with negative thoughts

Fear of rejection comes with a steady stream of negative thoughts. Thoughts about who you are, why you're not good enough and why you'll be pushed away. Thoughts that try to predict the future, telling you with absolute certainty that rejection is just around the corner. And thoughts about other people too, why they won't like you and why they'll turn away from you. When you follow those thoughts without questioning them, they pull you deeper into the fear.

Every time a situation triggers your fear of rejection, negative thoughts rush in on autopilot. Before you even realize it – bam, you're back in that space, thinking in ways that hurt you. These negative thoughts cloud your ability to see things clearly, making even neutral or slightly negative events feel like outright rejection. They don't help you feel good about yourself, and they definitely don't help you think clearly about who you are. And the more they come up, the more believable they become, because you're stuck in a loop. When thoughts like this have been around a long time they start to feel like the only way to think. If they stem from a past wound that still echoes in the present, your mind starts to act on that old pain. It expects the same thing to happen again and again, and that's what it will tell you too. It'll keep scanning for signs, looking out for those familiar patterns, even if they're not actually there.

How you relate to those thoughts matters a lot. The way you handle them can either give them more power or soften their hold. So, once you've made space to accept that these thoughts will show up the next step is to develop a gentle curiosity about them. With that curiosity, you can help your mind see more clearly. You can start to sift through what's really happening, what's not, and what's just a lingering echo, so you're not stuck reacting to the same old scripts every time. Here's a simple 4-step skill to help you notice and move through these thoughts:

Thought awareness and reframing

1. **Pause and acknowledge:** Take a moment to pause and notice the thoughts that are showing up. Acknowledge they're there and give yourself space to notice them.

2. **Note them down:** Write down the thoughts floating through your mind. What are they saying? For example: 'They didn't reply to my message, they must hate me.' Getting the thoughts on paper helps you see them clearly and creates some space between them and you.

3. **Get curious:** Take a closer look at those thoughts with curiosity, approaching them with a sense of openness. Here's some key questions to help you with that:

   - Is this thought 100% true?

   - If I had to convince a friend this thought was true, what solid proof would I have to show them?

   - Do I have any evidence that contradicts this thought?

   - Are there people who love and care about me who would disagree? What would they say?

   - What neutral explanations could there be? Are there other reasons I haven't considered, apart from them hating me or rejecting me? Maybe they didn't reply because they're busy, working, sick, distracted or something else.

   - If I didn't have a fear of rejection colouring my view, how would I see this?

   - How do people I know, who don't struggle with fear of rejection, usually handle situations like this?

4. **Reframe the thought:** Once you've sifted through what's really happening and what's not, and considered other possible explanations, take that original thought and reframe it into something more balanced, that's grounded in reality. For example:

   Original thought: 'They didn't reply to my message – they must hate me.'

   Reframed thought: 'I don't know why they haven't replied yet. There could be many reasons. I'll wait to hear back – they'll reply when they can.'

Reframing isn't about forced positivity or pretending everything's fine, it's about finding a perspective that's more accurate and more helpful. One that reflects reality and not fear. Here are some more examples to help you see this skill in action.

Reframing examples

Original thought: 'I'm going to be rejected.'
Reframed thought: 'Rejection is a possibility, but it's not a guarantee. Sometimes it happens for reasons that have nothing to do with me.'
Original thought: 'Everyone hates me.'
Reframed thought: 'I know people who like me, and I have experiences that show I'm valued.'
Original thought: 'People don't like me.'
Reframed thought: 'There are people who definitely like me, even if I sometimes doubt it.'
Original thought: 'Everyone reacts so negatively to me.'
Reframed thought: 'People generally have positive reactions to me, and when they don't, their reactions can be influenced by things that are unrelated to me.'
Original thought: 'They didn't like me; there's something wrong with me.'
Reframed thought: 'Nobody is liked by everyone – I don't even like everyone I meet, and that's okay. Sometimes, people just don't click, and that's normal.'
Original thought: 'They think I'm annoying.'
Reframed thought: 'I might worry that people find me annoying, but nobody has ever said that to me.'
Original thought: 'They stopped talking to me out of the blue, there must be something wrong with me.'

> **Reframed thought:** 'People often stop talking to you out of the blue when they lack the skills to communicate about things, or when something else is going on in their life.'

4. Stop self-rejecting

A fear of rejection can often be an outward manifestation of an inward battle with self-rejection. Like a lot of people, you might have a harsh, critical inner voice that's constantly picking you apart. That voice is its own form of rejection. It shows up in all the ways you put yourself down, expect failure, dwell on what you've done wrong and brush off anything you've done well, like it doesn't count. That steady flow of self-criticism rests on the painful belief that you're flawed and somehow deserving of being rejected. And when that becomes your default, constantly judging, criticizing and pulling yourself apart, you start to absorb the message that you are someone to be rejected. Even though it's the thing you're most afraid of, it begins to feel like something you should expect. Because if that's how you treat yourself, why would anyone else treat you differently?

That's why working through a fear of rejection on the outside also means changing how you treat yourself on the inside. It means shifting from repeating the old pattern of self-rejection to meeting yourself with compassion. Because self-compassion softens the voice of self-rejection, and it can help your brain respond in healthier ways. Every time you respond to yourself with warmth instead of criticism you're creating new neural pathways, ones that hold you in care instead of shame. And the more often you practise that, the less convincing it becomes that you're someone who's meant to be rejected.

And it's not just a mindset shift – it's physiological too. Harsh self-talk kicks your nervous system into overdrive. It sends the message that you're under threat, that something's wrong and your body gets flooded with anxiety, fear and tension. But self-compassion does the opposite: it switches on the calming centres in your brain. It helps soothe and regulate your nervous system. That compassion and kindness don't just feel good, they help your whole internal world function better, too.

And just to be clear – self-compassion isn't about pretending you don't have flaws, or trying to trick yourself into fake positivity. It means treating yourself like someone worth caring for. Someone you'd speak to with respect, patience and understanding, the same way you'd treat a friend. It's how you start to build a steady and solid inner foundation. One that makes rejection feel less threatening. And when it does happen, as it sometimes will, it won't hit as hard, because you're grounded in something stronger inside.

Here's a simple 4-step skill to help you shift out of self-rejection and into self-compassion:

The self-compassion switch

1. **Catch the Criticism**
   Every time you notice yourself saying something self-rejecting or judgemental, pause and note it down. Just catch it, that's your first step.

2. **Reword with Compassion**
   Now write down what you'd say instead, in the voice of someone who truly loves and cares about you. You don't

have to fully believe the words yet. You're just practising this new tone.

3. **Visualize the Voice**
   Sometimes it's easier to hear kind words when you imagine them coming from someone else. Picture a person whose care you trust, it could be a friend, a family member, someone warm and kind, and let yourself feel their words.

4. **Repeat and Repeat**
   Keep going. The more you do this, the more your brain starts to take it in. With practice, self-compassion starts to feel more familiar, believable and natural.

5. Take comfort in connection

Spend time with people who accept you and care about you, their presence can be especially comforting when your fear of rejection feels strong. Just being around them can remind you that the beliefs your fear sparks aren't always true. When you're feeling raw or vulnerable, lean into those relationships. Let them take the edges off your fear. If you want to, also talk to those people about what you're feeling, it can help you feel less alone and it can also lighten the emotional load. They might have a different perspective to offer you, too. One that challenges the stories your mind keeps replaying.

If you don't have a strong support network, I want you to know I see you, and I know what that feels like. Even without that circle, you can still give yourself something powerful: internal validation. Even without a support system, it's possible to build a sense of self-worth that doesn't have to depend on others. It starts with self-compassion, like we've talked about, and recognizing your own value. Journaling can really help too. Writing down your thoughts and feelings can help you unpack things, bringing some relief. If connection and a support system is something you really want, and feels like something you're missing, you can take small steps to find it and cultivate it. Think about the easiest places to start building those connections. You can start small with everyday moments, a conversation with a neighbour, a chat or coffee with someone at work or even just a few words to the person at your local shop. You could also consider joining an online community based on your interests, this can give you a shared starting point with others. And when you feel ready for a bit more, you can look into joining an in-person class or a club. These kinds of spaces, where you share interests can be fertile ground for genuine connection. And it's completely normal if it takes time to feel safe enough to open up, to trust, to accept care. That's not a flaw, that's a boundary, and a wise one. Your past experiences might make this feel difficult. Maybe they've taught you to be wary of others, or made it hard to believe that people can be safe. That can be part of why you feel alone now, because trust has been hard. But it doesn't mean connection is permanently out of reach. It just means you're protecting your heart because of what's happened, and that makes sense. So, it's okay, even recommended, to move slowly if you want to build connections. What matters is that you don't rule out the possibility of building something different, when you feel ready for it.

6. Redirection, not rejection

Now, let's turn to actual rejection, not just the fear of it. As you know, the fear often comes from having experienced rejection before. The way you handle it, how you process and react to it, can really determine how you move forward. And even though it hurts, rejection can actually be a valuable teacher. It can offer insights for growth or nudge you onto a path that fits you even better. In some situations, you might have the opportunity for external feedback, or you might need to turn inward and reflect to get that insight yourself by looking critically at what happened. There's a way to do this, and I'll show you how at the end of this section.

Rejection doesn't necessarily reflect your worth or your abilities, it often says more about timing, fit or external factors that are beyond your control. If you make it about your worth it will hold you back and feel like the end of the road. But the truth is rejection isn't a dead end, it can be a redirection that guides you towards something better, something different, or a new way of doing things.

Rejection isn't always personal

When we're rejected, our first instinct is to blame ourselves, and we often do that through a harsh lens. But that is never the full story. Can you honestly say it's all about you and who you are as a person? Is that the whole answer? You have to zoom out and think bigger and broader than just blaming yourself. Maybe you weren't the right fit, or maybe you haven't acquired the skills for this particular situation yet. Or maybe your goals didn't line up with what was at stake. Could it be that you were trying to fit a square peg into a round hole? Neither the peg nor the hole is wrong; they're just not compatible. If it was a friendship, maybe your interests had shifted, or your communication styles just never clicked. And, if you became friends by circumstance, like being in school together, over time, those differences created a distance, leading to a natural drifting apart.

The facts are your allies, so play detective. Look at all the information you have. What do the facts tell you? What was actually said? What was the feedback? By focusing on the facts, you can move away from self-criticism and into a more objective understanding of what you felt.

Here are some more questions to help you reflect on your experience of rejection, so you can see things from different angles and carry those insights with you.

Reflection for redirection

- Rejection only happens when you're brave enough to try. So, what strengths – like courage, determination or openness – did you show by putting yourself out there?
- What did this experience teach you about yourself, others or life in general?
- Every experience offers a lesson if we're open to it. What does this tell you about what you could do differently next time? Could a different approach work? Or maybe a different person, opportunity or environment?
- Finally, what can you take from this experience to motivate yourself in moving forward?

Before we move onto our final skill, I'd like to share a personal story with you. I took a gap year before university because I wanted to travel and also needed to save some money, so I looked for jobs that could give me both. I applied to be an air stewardess, drawn in by the idea of seeing beautiful parts of the world. Despite my excitement (and thinking I looked the part in an iconic pink pinstripe suit from Bay Trading – if you know, you know!) I didn't make it through the interviews. I was rejected and it stung. I started questioning why I wasn't good enough. I thought I was smart and could do anything, having just finished A-levels in biology, chemistry and physics. Still wanting to travel, I then, quite laughably, applied to be an air traffic controller abroad – also unsurprisingly unsuccessful. Looking back, though, I'm grateful for those rejections. They were a redirection, leading me away from paths that weren't right for me. Instead, I ended up doing incredibly rewarding work in a mother-and-baby unit as a support worker, along with helping people with Alzheimer's and victims of domestic violence. Those rejections led me to the path I was always meant to be on – helping others. And to this day, I'm so thankful for where I am now, walking that path every day. Sometimes a door closing isn't the end, it's life gently steering you towards something better suited to you.

7. Let your values lead you past fear

A fear of rejection makes you want to avoid anything that could lead to it, and this is completely human. But often that fear starts calling the shots, shaping what you go after and what you don't. And it doesn't take long before the things that really matter, the things you value end up on the back seat. Because fear has convinced you it's safer not to try than to risk being rejected. And this kind of avoidance shows up in so many different ways. Maybe you stay quiet in moments when you actually want to speak up. You might hold back from saying out loud what you really think. You might avoid going after an opportunity you really want. You might keep your distance in relationships or bend to meet other people's expectations. And while all this might help you avoid potential rejection, it also pulls you away from your values, from being fully yourself and living your life on your terms. Fear becomes the compass instead of your values.

But there's another way, a better way, where you can choose to act from your values, even when fear is there. You don't have to get rid of fear completely to make those moves towards your values. It's about letting fear be there without letting it call the shots. You learn to walk alongside it by following your values, rather than letting it lead you.

So take a moment to reconnect with your values, the kind of person you are, and the life you want to live, even in those moments that feel hard. Think about how your values can guide your choices even when fear is present. Pick out your value, and then ask yourself: 'If I were taking action in line with this value, even with my fear of rejection in the background, what would I be doing?' Then do this for all your values.

I've included some values below, along with some action pointers to help you see how making decisions from your values, rather than your fear, can change the way you show up.

Value	Action
Authenticity	Being true to yourself in what you say and do, even when fear of rejection is sitting in the background. That fear might still be there, but you don't let it dictate your direction. You act from your values, not from the pull to fit in or win approval. And that choice builds a deeper self-acceptance. You're not trying to be someone else, you're trying to be you. And that's what creates real connection with people who see and value the real you.
Connection	You care about connection, so you take steps to build it, even if that means being more vulnerable. You understand that rejection is part of the deal when it comes to human relationships. But you're choosing real connection over the safety of holding back or pretending, because the value of connection built on who you really are is worth the risk.

Courage	Courage means showing up, even when it's uncomfortable. It's choosing to take the step, even with the fear of being turned down. You don't need the fear to disappear, you just need to act in spite of it. And every time you do, it gets a little easier. That's how you build strength and stay true to the value of courage.
Growth	You don't treat rejection like failure, you treat it like feedback. Sometimes it hurts, for sure. But you look at it with curiosity. What can I learn here? What could I do differently next time? Or maybe it's just accepting that this is life nudging you in a new direction. Either way, you take it as part of the path to growing, and not a stop sign.
Open-mindedness	Even when fear's in the mix, you stay open, to people, ideas, situations, anything. Including the messy and surprising parts of life. You'd rather be stretched by something new than shrink away from it. Because living a meaningful life means being willing to feel uncomfortable sometimes in the pursuit of staying open-minded.
Flexibility	Rejection doesn't mean stop – it means shift, adapt or change. Flexibility is about adjusting, not about giving up. Maybe you try again, or try differently. Maybe you take a new path altogether. Either way, you keep moving. You don't get stuck in fear. You keep moving forward with flexibility, learning to manoeuvre through the unexpected twists and turns that come up along the way.

When you live in line with your values, you're not just telling yourself your worth matters, you're showing the world that what matters to you is important enough to embody, and it's how you choose to live. As you keep walking this path, your confidence grows, and so does your resilience. You'll start to feel more at ease with who you are, and that fear of rejection won't carry as much weight. Why? Because your sense of worth is no longer tied to how others might react to you. Instead, it's rooted in living by what truly matters to you, the values you've chosen. And that's more solid and reliable than anyone else's opinion.

Things to hold onto . . .

Rejection is a completely normal part of life, something everyone experiences and survives, often many times over.

Rejection is not just about someone saying 'no' to you. It can also show up as a fear of not being liked, not fitting in, being judged or being treated in ways that make you feel like you don't matter.

A fear of rejection can surface in all kinds of relationships, including friendships, family dynamics and work. And in today's world, that includes the digital space too.

You can break free from the fear of rejection by using skills like acceptance, processing your feelings and the thoughts that come up. You can also learn to stop rejecting yourself and start choosing self-compassion instead.

And your values can help, too. They give you something steady to act on, a way to make decisions based on what actually matters to you, instead of letting fear make those choices for you.

Part Four

Protecting Your Peace with Boundaries

Has someone ever asked you a question that made you feel exposed, vulnerable or uncomfortable? It could be a question like, 'Why are you so quiet?' or 'So, tell me about your trauma.' These kinds of questions intrude on deeply personal issues. Then there are questions about other aspects of your personal life like, 'How much money do you make?' or 'Why don't you have kids?' These also stir up emotion; they can feel like such an invasion. There are also judgemental questions like, 'What's your body count?' – referring to how many people you've slept with! Or 'Why are you dressed like that?' These scrutinize you or make you feel judged for choices that are really nobody else's business. Sometimes people ask invasive questions because they don't understand the importance of boundaries themselves, but it can also come from malice, a desire for control or a sense of entitlement to push you for information they know is uncomfortable for you. But they disregard that and intrude into the private space of your life that doesn't belong to them and where they have no place.

Boundary violations aren't just limited to questions, though. They can also be violations of your emotional boundaries, your physical boundaries, your space, your time, energy, your financial boundaries and so much more. It's everywhere you want to have a limit, which then gets crossed or disregarded. It might be somebody taking up your time and mental space by bombarding you with messages and phone calls when you don't want them to. They might do this because of their own issues or insecurities, but that doesn't give them the right to violate your boundaries by making their need for reassurance your responsibility instead of dealing with their own problems. It can also happen when you ask someone to stop doing or saying something because it makes you uncomfortable, yet they ignore you and keep doing it anyway. It can be physical as well, when someone is a bit too close, or touchy, whether at work, in friendships or in family life – like being forced to hug relatives even when you don't want to. It can also be when you communicate that an expectation is causing you anxiety, but they persist regardless, ignoring your limits and pushing their own desire over your mental health. Or it can be making inappropriate comments, sharing your secrets, constantly interrupting you, not letting you speak, asking you for money – the list goes on. Boundary violations can also involve a lack of privacy, having your personal space or belongings searched through without your permission, sometimes even without your knowledge. Or even having your things taken without your permission.

Chapter 1:
What Are Boundaries?

Now that you've got a clear picture of boundary violations, let's define what boundaries actually are. Simply put, boundaries are your absolute RIGHT. They are the limits, guidelines or personal rules you set for yourself in all areas of your life to define what's acceptable to you in relation to your personal space, emotions, thoughts and actions, as well as how others behave towards you. Boundaries are about what you will and won't do.[13] Boundaries also define what's yours and what belongs to others, not just in terms of material items, but also in emotional, mental and physical ways. Boundaries protect your well-being by determining how you act, how you treat yourself and how you allow others to treat you. Boundaries are also all about respecting each other's comfort zones and privacy. Boundaries are a form of self-respect and self-care. Even though boundaries are limits, they're actually liberating. Having boundaries doesn't mean you're restricting yourself; it means you're protecting yourself.

All of this might sound clear in theory, but boundaries can still feel abstract because they're invisible and internal. To make them easier to grasp, it can help to have a metaphor or mental image that represents them. When you can visualize your boundaries, they feel more real, it's like knowing exactly where your fence or lock is. That image can give you a sense of security and confidence for when you need to hold your ground. You can visualize boundaries in many different ways. As a door to your home, you get to decide who's allowed in, for how long and what for. Or as a personal, un-burstable bubble that is protecting your comfort zone. If visual representations help you, you can come up with an image that represents boundaries for you. Hold that image in mind as you read this chapter, it can make your boundaries feel more real and easier to hold.

Chapter 2: Why Setting Boundaries Feels So Hard

Setting boundaries can feel like an uphill struggle. Even when you know it's the right thing to do, it can be hard – and for lots of understandable reasons. If you grew up without clear examples of what healthy boundaries looked like, you might feel uncertain about them. Maybe the adults around you never modelled them well, or maybe your definition of a boundary has been fuzzy. Because boundaries are about protecting or meeting your needs, you have to actually know what those needs are. If no one taught you how to identify your needs – or you don't know how to figure them out – then knowing where to draw the line becomes almost impossible. You can't set a limit if you don't know where it needs to be.

In some cases, even when you're clear on what you need, it doesn't automatically mean that setting boundaries will be easy. Because, sometimes, just the idea of protecting that need can stir up fear and anxiety. That fear might come from rejection, conflict, tension, about people being angry or disappointed in you, or something else. If you've tried to set boundaries before and had those fears confirmed, it might have left a lasting imprint. One that tells you, don't do that again it's not worth the fallout. Sometimes, just the anticipation of those reactions can feel scarier than the consequences of not having boundaries at all. So staying as you are can feel safer, but often comes at a cost.

But fear isn't the only thing that holds people back. Sometimes, it's the belief that you don't even deserve to set boundaries. That's where low self-esteem comes in – it convinces you that your needs don't matter enough to be protected. When you don't feel worthy, it's easy to believe you don't matter, and if you don't matter, why would you bother protecting yourself with boundaries? Why would you feel entitled to set them? Some people think they have to build up their self-worth before they can start asserting limits. But the truth is, it often works the other way around. When you act like you matter – by setting boundaries – you start to feel like you do matter. Bit by bit, boundaries help reinforce a sense of self-worth, because they're proof that you're willing to show up for yourself.

Guilt is another obstacle that can creep in. Especially if you've grown up believing that others come first. If taking care of yourself is unfamiliar, setting boundaries might also feel selfish. But here's something to think about, boundaries aren't about shutting people out – they're about protecting the version of you that can show up for others in a way that feels genuine. When you think of boundaries as an act of self-care, they stop being something you feel guilty about and start becoming something you feel grounded by.

Many of the challenges with boundaries come from family dynamics, where there can be layers of complexity. In some families, it's not just that boundaries were unclear – it's that there was an unspoken rule that, because of the biological tie, anyone could ask anything of anyone, at any time. And everyone was expected to comply. These dynamics aren't always obvious. Sometimes they show up in subtle ways: that quiet expectation that you shouldn't question things, disrupt the peace or rock the boat. Even if that means sacrificing your autonomy for the sake of keeping everyone else comfortable. But that's not right, and it's certainly not healthy. Just because someone is 'family' it doesn't mean they should get unlimited access to your time, your energy or your emotional bandwidth. In fact, because family dynamics are so layered, emotionally charged and complex they often require the clearest of boundaries.

When unhealthy family dynamics shape your early relationships, they also lead to another pattern, where you confuse empathy with responsibility. Empathy is a beautiful thing, but when it's not paired with boundaries, it can become a toxic and draining cycle that you get stuck in. You try to fix other people's problems as if they're your own, while they don't take the same responsibility, so nothing really changes for them. And because you still feel responsible, and haven't drawn a clear boundary, you keep trying. It doesn't work – and in the process of trying it wears you down. It's like patching up someone else's broken walls while never building any of your own. Fixing other people doesn't fix them, and it won't fix you. Without boundaries, the effort you pour into others can end up hurting both of you.

And there's also trauma – probably one of the most powerful forces of all when it comes to boundaries. Trauma almost always involves some form of boundary violation – whether physical, emotional or psychological. And that kind of violation can shake your sense of what boundaries are. It can leave you unsure about whether you're allowed to have them, or how to set and maintain them, and what to do when someone crosses them. When boundary violations have been part of your past, they can feel familiar – sometimes even normal, like it's just how things are supposed to be. But it isn't, and the truth is, you always deserve to be protected.

Chapter 3:
The Cost of Living Without Boundaries

Living without boundaries comes at a cost that can drain your well-being. Every time you neglect a boundary, you pay a hidden cost, and over time it can accumulate and have a big impact. Having no boundaries disrupts the balance between what you need and what others need. It makes you more reactive instead of proactive; you're so busy responding to external demands that there's no room left for you. You can become chronically stressed, and when you do, you can lose the ability to discern what really matters to you; you waste a lot of time and energy on autopilot, instead of doing things that align with your values. Your relationships can also become unbalanced, with resentment, bitterness, conflict and unmet needs festering beneath the surface until, one day, they become too much.

This lack of control of your life can make you feel overwhelmed. You don't have the energy to replenish your resources; you can feel hopeless and depressed. And the more vulnerable you become, the more unable you are to focus on your growth. A lack of boundaries also makes you an easy target for being mistreated by others. You risk adopting other people's goals and opinions as your own.[14] People with toxic traits will take advantage of your willingness, degrading your self-esteem even further. As your self-esteem plummets, there can be an almost constant whisper in your mind that you don't matter, and in those rare moments when you feel like you do, you end up feeling guilty for taking actions that you absolutely should to prioritize yourself. Without boundaries, you're on a runaway roller coaster, careening through life with no control through emotional extremes, where every twist and turn can catch you off guard.

If your boundaries at work are poor, you're never truly present in your professional or personal life; it's like living in two worlds at once, but never being fully in one place. You might start second-guessing yourself and feeling like an impostor. Poor boundaries at work have been linked to burn-out, and symptoms like exhaustion, detachment and feeling ineffective. The research also shows that when people actively set and maintain boundaries, it helps buffer against burnout and helps their overall well-being.[15] When your work life bleeds into your personal life, it doesn't just leave you drained though, it can also erode your happiness.[16] Boundaries also affect how you manage your time. When you don't have them, it's hard to know how much time you consciously want to give to certain things – or to notice where your time is really going. And the same goes for money, without clear boundaries around it, it can feel like there's never enough. The anxiety, overwhelm, panic and depression that come with financial instability are in a league of their own. Your body also speaks up when your boundaries are missing. This might show up in poor sleep, your physical health, your fitness levels or in the quiet toll your emotions take.

At some point in life, we've all been in at least one of these places. It doesn't have to stay like that: you can learn to set boundaries, even if you've never had them before, or if you've lost touch with them. You can start building those protective walls around you. Creating a home for yourself. A safe space where you feel secure. Where your relationships are genuine, your needs are met, your work life is rewarding, your personal time is fulfilling, your physical health improves and you have time for personal growth, and time for rest. Let's start building that home in the next chapter!

Chapter 4: How to Define and Set Your Boundaries

In this chapter, you'll learn some powerful tools for setting your boundaries. Take it one step at a time, and absorb these tools gradually, at a pace that works for you. Start with what's easiest, build your confidence and then keep going. Because setting boundaries can feel complicated, I've laid out a step-by-step approach to make it easier. In reality, it's not always going to follow this exact order; it'll be more fluid, with some trial and error mixed in too. I've laid it out like this so you have a clear framework to start with that helps you craft the bigger picture of your boundaries. If you're new to setting boundaries or face an unfamiliar situation, there will be moments when you misjudge, hesitate or realize what you wanted afterwards; that's normal. It's exactly how you learn more about your limits; each experience, especially the tricky ones, teaches you something that helps you set better boundaries next time.

1. Know your needs and build your boundaries

Before you can define your limits, you have to know what you actually need – what nourishes you, what drains you, and what makes you feel safe, respected and valued. When you know your needs, your boundaries are more meaningful and will create the space for you to thrive. For example, recognizing you need time to recharge after work, makes it easier to set boundaries around your evening time. Or, if financial security is important to you, understanding that lending money compromises this can help you set limits on when and how much you give.

You can break your needs down into different areas of your life:

1. **Physical boundaries:** These boundaries are about taking care of your physical needs and feeling safe in your body. Do you feel comfortable with hugs from everyone? Do you get enough sleep, do you eat well?

2. **Emotional boundaries:** These help you keep your feelings separate from others, so you're not overloaded by them. It's also about deciding who you share your vulnerable side with, when and how much of it.

3. **Time boundaries:** These are about balancing work, rest, hobbies and relationships. It's saying no when you need to, so you have enough time for yourself and you don't burn out.

4. **Mental boundaries:** These protect your headspace. For instance, choosing what conversations you engage in or what information you want to express.

5. **Material boundaries:** These are about your stuff! How you feel about lending or sharing things. Setting material boundaries helps you decide when and how to do that without compromising yourself.

6. **Relational boundaries:** Whether it's family, friends or colleagues, healthy relationships need limits too. These

are about defining what feels good, safe and respectful in your connections.

7. **Digital/Technology boundaries:** These are about setting boundaries around screen time and social media.

As well as thinking through different areas of your life, you can also use these questions to get insights into your needs:

- What needs to change for you to meet your needs?
- What do you need to step back from?
- What do you want to do more of?
- Who do you want to be around, and who do you want to see less of?
- When do you feel your best or worst?
- What makes you feel comfortable, and what feels uncomfortable?
- What makes you feel resentful?

Another way to get insight into your needs is to think about the patterns in your daily life. Pay close attention to where things aren't going the way you need in any area and where making changes could help you feel better. For example, you might notice issues with time-related boundaries if you stay up too late replying to messages or with physical boundaries if you're not getting enough sleep. Maybe you don't stop to eat on time, or you spend too long on calls with others when instead you need to focus on getting things done that make your life easier.

Once you have clarity on your needs, you can use them to create clear, actionable boundaries. What limit do you need in place to protect each need? Writing a simple sentence for each one can make it easier to hold onto internally and express it when you need to. Here are some examples:

Physical boundaries

- 'I like hugs, but only from people I feel comfortable with.'
- 'I don't want to be touched without being asked.'
- 'I need time to rest and recharge, so I will prioritize getting enough sleep.'

Emotional boundaries

- 'I love deep conversations, but I also need space to talk about fun things.'
- 'There are some topics I can't talk about when I'm stressed or overwhelmed.'
- 'I need to help the people I care about, without taking on their problems too much.'

Time boundaries

- 'I need to make time for things that make me happy, like reading and walking.'
- 'I need my evenings for myself.'
- 'I can't take phone calls after 9 p.m.'

Mental boundaries

- 'I don't have to stay engaged in debates that drain me, I can stop.'
- 'I enjoy hearing different perspectives but I don't have to take them on as my own.'

- 'I need to protect my peace by limiting how much negative news and social media I consume.'

Material boundaries

- 'I can't lend money right now, but I'm happy to offer other support.'
- 'I take care of my belongings and only share them when I feel comfortable.'
- 'I budget for generosity, so I can give in a way that feels good and sustainable.'

Relational boundaries

- 'I value thoughtful advice, but only when I ask for it.'
- 'I need to make my own decisions in relationships.'
- 'I need to be around people who respect me.'

Digital boundaries

- 'I won't check emails after a certain time.'
- 'I need to make space for real-life connections by putting my phone away during meals.'
- 'I want to limit my screen time to a set number of minutes or hours each day.'

Setting boundaries isn't a one-time thing; it's something that evolves with you, as your life changes, as you have new experiences and meet new people. Nor can you predict all your boundaries in advance; there's no such thing as having a pre-written list of limits for every situation you encounter. Some boundaries only become clear once we go through an experience. As you move through life, new relationships, friendships, jobs and challenges will shape your needs. And you might find you need to adjust your limits – perhaps needing a stronger boundary in one area or a more flexible one in another. Always listen to your feelings to pick up on discomfort, resentment or feeling drained. These can be your inner signals that a boundary is missing or needs reinforcing. Sometimes, you won't realize you need a boundary until it's already been crossed. It happens. The important thing is to reflect on it afterwards and ask yourself: 'What would my boundary have been?' And do things differently next time. Each experience you go through helps you understand yourself better so you can fine-tune your limits and keep cultivating them so they support you.

2. Find your way through your feelings

Intense emotions often stand in the way of what we want to do, and that's precisely what can happen when you try to set boundaries. You're not just avoiding the action of setting the boundary itself, you don't want to feel the emotions that come with doing so. You don't like those feelings, and you don't know how to handle them. It's the main reason that many people struggle to set boundaries; they dislike those feelings of awkwardness, unease or guilt. It's completely natural to have these kinds of feelings, especially when you're doing something new and challenging. Letting your emotions stand in the way of setting boundaries won't get you where you want to be. What will help is learning to process these emotions so they become less intense, allowing you to feel more confident in setting the limits you want. To process these feelings, you have to really feel them. You can do that with the 'Feel Your Feelings' 5 Cs exercise I introduced in Part 3 (see p. 69) to help you work through difficult emotions. Here's a recap of how you can do that – in the form of an example:

Capture: 'I'm feeling guilty and awkward.'

Connect: 'My jaw is tight, and my stomach feels so knotted.'

Curiosity: 'I'm thinking I'm a bad friend, and they are angry at me. My mind is telling me I should have just lent them the money, then I wouldn't have to feel so bad.'

Calm: 'It's okay to feel guilty. Setting boundaries is hard. I made a decision that was right for me, and that's valid. I'm allowed to protect my financial well-being. I can be a good friend and still have boundaries. I can go for a walk to release some of the tension I feel.'

Choose: 'I value financial security and healthy boundaries, so I acted in line with those values. I also value my friendship, so I'll message them to let them know I'm here for them and can help them in other ways.'

3. Ditch the auto YES!

Stop saying yes without thinking. If you're saying yes on autopilot, you're not giving yourself the chance to figure out what you really want to happen first. Breaking the habit of the automatic yes makes space for the things that matter to you. Every yes is a commitment, and if you're not careful, it can mean overcommitting yourself and putting your own needs last. I'm not talking about the yeses that are small, joyful things which improve your well-being; I'm talking about the automatic, unconsidered yeses. Those are the ones that can be problematic. It's the big, frequent ones or the ones from certain people that you might need to watch out for more. Not every single request needs a full internal review, though. Sometimes, a quick yes is perfectly fine and healthy. Other times, it's helpful to tune into how you feel about the request and only say yes if it feels right. This can help you avoid resentment towards the person asking and towards yourself for agreeing to something you didn't want to do. So, make a commitment now to ditch the auto yes. The next time someone asks you to do something, and you feel that knee-jerk yes about to slip out, pause. Instead of defaulting to yes, have a few go-to responses ready. Here are three to get you started:

> 'I need to check, I'll get back to you later.'
> 'I'm not sure if I can, let me think about it.'
> 'I'll have to get back to you on that.'

4. Boundary-setting visualization

Sometimes it can feel impossible to imagine ourselves setting boundaries, especially when doing so feels new. People say, 'Oh, I could never say that.' But just because something feels out of reach now it doesn't mean it always will be. A powerful tool for bridging that gap is visualization, which can be used as a mental rehearsal to practise handling situations that need boundaries before they happen. In this kind of visualization, you picture the worst-case scenario as well as things working out exactly as you want them to. It's about exploring all possibilities, so when the real-life moment comes you're not stepping into a complete unknown. Because you've already been there in your mind it makes it feel less daunting, and more doable. So here's a visualization to help you practise setting boundaries that might feel too scary right now. Find a quiet, comfortable place where you won't be disturbed. Sit or lie down comfortably, close your eyes and take a few deep breaths, slowly in through your nose and out through your mouth. Let your body relax.

Picture yourself in a situation where you're afraid to set

a boundary. Notice who else is with you. Pay attention to what they look like. How they sound. What they're wearing. How they're standing, or are they sitting? How many people are there? Notice as much detail about them as you can. Also notice what time of day it is. Take in as much detail as you can about your surroundings. Where are you? Let your mind explore the space around you. Notice the colours, the sounds in the background. Pay attention to any textures, the smells in the atmosphere. Let yourself fully be in this moment.

Next, imagine yourself setting the boundary with them, and it going well, feeling easy. Hear your voice in a calm, steady and clear tone. Picture the other person's response. They accept your boundary with understanding. Maybe they look a little surprised, but they remain respectful. Notice how it feels in your body to stand your ground with confidence. Take a deep breath in through your nose, and again slowly exhale through your mouth. Settle into this image of yourself. Saying to yourself: 'I am strong. I can do this.' Repeat this a few times, letting confidence take root within you.

Now, let's imagine the situation not going as planned. This time the other person reacts negatively, in the ways that you fear. Maybe they disagree, dismiss your feelings, challenge your boundary or push back in another way. Again, just see their reaction, hear their words, notice their facial expression and their body language. Even if it makes you uncomfortable, stay with it. Notice what you're doing too, and how you're reacting to them being like this.

To finish off, go back to the picture of yourself handling it exactly as you'd like to in real life. You're calm and confident. You don't panic, backtrack, or over-explain yourself. You hold your boundary with confidence, speaking firmly but kindly. You know deep down that you don't need their approval, you just need to honour what feels right for you.

Take a few more deep breaths and let this final positive image of things working out settle into your mind. When you're ready, open your eyes and slowly bring yourself back to the present moment.

5. Body boundaries

People often struggle with knowing how to respond when their personal space or body boundaries are crossed. I'm talking about those moments when someone stands too close to you, leans on you, or touches you in another way when you don't want them to. Those small but very uncomfortable intrusions that catch you off guard, they can almost shock you, leaving you unsure of what to do.

What makes this even more complicated is the past, especially if you've ever been violated by someone's touch in any way. Physical touch can feel unwanted for so many reasons. Maybe it brings up painful memories. Maybe it feels overwhelming because of sensory sensitivities. Maybe you're worried about germs or cleanliness. Or maybe, it's as simple as this – you just don't like being touched. And that's reason enough; not that you need a reason.

It can also be harder to assert body boundaries if you grew up in a home where you were told to give family members a hug or a kiss when you didn't want to. Those memories of shrinking inside yourself not knowing if you had the right to say no, or even how to say it, can stay with you. It teaches you, in subtle ways, that speaking up to unwanted touch is wrong. What children should be taught instead is that it's okay to say no to any kind of touch, even if it's from a family member who wants affection. Too often, children are told to offer touch to meet an adult's need for affection, or for politeness. But who is that really for? It's about meeting the adult's needs.

And that's completely the wrong way round. Children aren't here to meet adults' needs, it's the other way round. Teaching children that they can set those boundaries is essential for their autonomy and safety. When that isn't taught as a child it can affect how you handle things as an adult. In uncomfortable situations, you're not just dealing with what's happening now, you're also carrying the pain of those past uncomfortable experiences. And that can make an awkward moment feel even harder to deal with.

I was recently on a packed train; the seat next to me was empty and later in the journey a man came and sat down beside me. At first, he stayed on his side, but gradually he started leaning closer and closer to me, until his whole side was pressed against mine. There was an armrest between us, and you could clearly see where the two seats met, defining my space and his space. I turned to him, and with a firm voice said, 'Excuse me, can you stop leaning on me?' I said it loud enough for others to hear, because knowing that others know what's happening can boost your sense of safety and it can give you that extra confidence. In that moment I also wanted to normalize standing up for yourself in public, so wanted others to hear. He immediately moved away, creating space between the two of us; in fact he turned his back to me and faced the aisle, leaving a big gap between us.

I'm sharing this to show you that, sometimes, it takes just one sentence to reset a boundary. You don't have to overthink it. You definitely don't have to justify it. A short, simple, direct statement works well. Yes, it might feel awkward in the moment, but remember your comfort matters more than someone else's temporary embarrassment or need to invade your space. Your body belongs to you. And you deserve to feel safe and comfortable in whatever space you're in. You get to choose who touches you and who doesn't. Saying no to unwanted touch isn't rude or selfish. It's self-respect, and it's essential self-care.

Here are some things you can say to set boundaries around your body:

> 'Please don't touch me.'
>
> 'Stop touching me.'
>
> 'I need space, please move back.'
>
> 'Please keep your hands to yourself.'
>
> 'I'm not a huggy person.'

Bonus boundary phrases

Just before we wrap up this section, here are some extra phrases to help you set boundaries across the different areas we've explored. These might also inspire you to create your own phrases.

For your personal space

> 'Can I get a bit more space between us, please?'
>
> 'Ooh I need a bit more personal space than this.'
>
> 'Ugh, I'm so hot, please can you move back.'
>
> 'I think we might be closer than a tin of sardines right now, let's make some room!'

For your physical and emotional needs

> 'I'm so tired, I need to rest.'
>
> 'I need some time to myself for [eating, sleeping, exercise or another need].'

'I need time to process this.'

'I can't do this right now.'

'I can't handle this, it's too much for me.'

For refusing unwanted topics of conversation

'I don't want to discuss politics/religion [or whatever topic you don't want to discuss].'

'That's too personal for me to talk about.'

'I'm not comfortable talking about that.'

For unwanted advice and opinions

'I need to make up my own mind about this.'

'I appreciate your opinion, but I'll figure it out.'

For refusing participation in something

'I am not taking part in that.'

'I can't do that'

'Count me out.'

For conversations and in relationships

'I feel like my feelings aren't being considered, so I can't continue this conversation.'

'I've said all I need to say for now.'

'I can't control how you feel.'

'I won't be spoken to like that.'

'I'm not being difficult, I'm just taking care of myself.'

'I'm sorry you feel that way, but I need to do what's right for me.'

'I disagree with that, but I'm not going to argue.'

'I know how I've acted, and I'm comfortable with it.'

'This conversation isn't going anywhere productive. I need to excuse myself.'

Chapter 5: People's Reactions to Your Boundaries

When you set boundaries, you will get a range of reactions; it all depends on who you're dealing with and how they feel about your limits. The reactions can be positive or negative, depending on the person's personality, emotional intelligence and the quality of the relationship you have with them. Some people will understand, accept and respect your boundaries because they genuinely care about you. You might not run into any issues with those people because they're psychologically healthy. In fact, they might even admire your boundaries. They might feel genuinely happy that you're finding healthier ways to deal with life, relieved even, because they care about you and have watched you struggle in the past by giving or allowing too much.

Some people might feel confused about why you're setting boundaries, and how your new boundaries might affect their relationship with you. They might worry that the dynamics will change. Some people might not even notice or be affected by the changes you make. Which can be a helpful reminder that we often overestimate how much others are thinking about our decisions and actions. Others may simply be curious, wondering what's behind your new boundaries. They might want to understand why you're making these changes, and maybe even feel inspired by them. It might get them thinking about their own boundaries.

Then there are also the people who might not like you setting boundaries for whatever reason. Maybe because they don't want you to change, it makes them uncomfortable. If they benefited from your lack of boundaries it now means they won't be able to. If this is the case, it's more about them struggling to separate what is personally important to them and not quite understanding why your boundaries are equally important to you. Even when people have these negative reactions, some of them may eventually adjust to your new way of being and, over time, you could end up having a healthier relationship with them. Others might take your boundaries personally, feeling offended by them, and they could even respond negatively to them.

They might say things like: 'Why are you doing this, I've done nothing wrong,' trying to make you feel like you're the problem. This is often a way to make you question whether you should even set a boundary. They might say, 'You're overreacting,' minimizing your feelings to make you feel like your boundaries aren't needed. Or they might say, 'After all I've done for you,' an emotional guilt trip, trying to use your history against you to make you feel like you owe them. They might say, 'You're being selfish,' accusing you for prioritizing your needs in order to guilt you into backing down. Or it could be, 'If you really cared about me, you wouldn't do this,' which is emotional manipulation, trying to misuse your compassion as a way to get you to drop your boundaries. Then there's also, 'Who do you think you are?' Challenging your right to assert yourself as if you need permission to have a say in your life.

Here are a couple of example responses for any one of these:

'I'm not being difficult. I'm just setting a boundary that's important for me.'

'I'm sorry you feel that way, but this is how I need to take care of myself.'

It's not just words that you'll encounter; some people might distance themselves. Or they might completely cut ties with you because the dynamic they once relied on to get their way no longer exists. This kind of silence can speak volumes, feeling like a quiet disapproval. When someone reacts strongly to a boundary you set, whether it's anger, guilt or defensiveness, it often points to them struggling with the idea that you have needs separate from theirs. They might feel like your needs are somehow threatening their own, as if your space makes theirs feel smaller. And that can be confusing, even painful. It can make you question the relationship, but try to remember that their reaction is more about their perspective than the validity of your boundary. If you think back on the relationship, you might be able to see that there were things going on underneath all along. Maybe there was tension, an imbalance of some kind or unease that was there long before you set your boundary. Those issues felt manageable, even tolerable, but only because you kept accommodating them. And, now they're surfacing, not because you created them but because you finally drew a line.

It's normal to find yourself wondering why they are acting this way. Why does it feel so hard for them to accept your limits? The truth is, the 'why' behind their behaviour isn't the most important thing; it's their reaction that tells you what you need to know. Their unwillingness to respect your needs and limits can be a red flag. It could also be a sign that they lack empathy for you, while at the same time feeling deep empathy for themselves, seeing their needs and entitlement to you as more important than what you want or need. Not only that: by reacting negatively, they're also punishing you for setting your boundaries.

If things escalate into an unproductive back-and-forth debate, instead of getting drawn in you can say something like, 'This isn't productive,' 'I can't do this,' or 'I need to go now,' and then leave the conversation. Sometimes, these aren't really conversations at all, they're attempts to wear you down, criticize you, challenge your authority or to pull you into another unhealthy dynamic. Don't accept the invitation to replay the same old patterns with that person. This time, you can turn that invitation down. Ending that conversation is also a boundary, and it's yours to set.

When someone who's hurt you by reacting negatively to your boundaries comes back with a sincere apology and real empathy, you can decide whether you want to continue the relationship. If you do, also think about the boundaries that will make it the kind of relationship that allows both of you to experience it at its best.

Lastly, for those people that you may have known well or for a long time, who have cut you out of their life after you set a boundary, take a moment to ask yourself: is this really a relationship worth pouring more of your energy into? If they've chosen to distance themselves rather than meet you with understanding or respect, it's a sign that the relationship would not have been sustainable. I know it's tempting to reach out and try to fix things, especially when that empathetic side of you, the one who didn't set those boundaries in the first place, wants to make things right. But the healthiest and most loving thing you can do for yourself is to let go of unhealthy relationships. If there's no reciprocity, it's time to let it go; honouring your boundaries is the truest path to your peace and growth.

Things to hold onto . . .

Boundaries are an absolute right that every single one of us has. They're your personal limits, your guidelines, your rules for what feels okay and what doesn't in all areas of your life. Boundaries help you define what's acceptable when it comes to your space, your emotions, your thoughts, your time, your actions and how others treat you.

Even though boundaries are limits, they're actually freeing. They're a form of self-respect – a way to protect your peace and create safety for yourself.

It can be hard to set boundaries if you've never been shown how, or if deep down you don't believe you matter enough to have them. Or if you struggle with guilt, or you grew up in an environment where boundaries weren't modelled to you.

You can define and set boundaries at any point in your life. It starts with knowing your needs, then creating limits that protect and honour them.

Part Five

Assertiveness

Selena told me about something she witnessed at the airport that left an impression on her. She was standing in line, and a man was trying to push his way to the front of a queue. Selena told me that the woman in front of her turned to him and said, 'Excuse me, there's a queue. You can line up at the back.' When he ignored her, she became louder and said: 'Stop pushing in! You need to wait like everyone else.' People heard and turned to look, the man backed off and joined the back of the line. Selena described how her heart was pounding just watching it happen. She said just imagining herself being that assertive made her cringe – but deep down, that was exactly the kind of confidence she wished she had.

Like many people, Selena freezes the moment someone crosses a line. She told me: 'It's like a wave of anger rises up in me, but instead of doing anything, I squash it back down. Then I spend hours replaying it in my head, annoyed at myself for staying quiet and being such a walkover. But at the same time, I don't even know if I want to say something, because I don't want to upset people. I can't stand the thought of it all. But I also can't stand not being assertive. I wish I could handle situations like that with a bit of confidence – like that woman had. I want to be able to speak up without hesitating or feeling scared.'

I've heard the same struggle from others too – like Frankie, who said she pushes her feelings down and doesn't speak up even when something feels totally unfair. Or Bailey, who stews over things that have happened and only thinks of the right thing to say hours later. Or Nadine, who gets so anxious and feels so awkward trying to be assertive that her words come out wrong. They all want the same thing, to be able to speak up for themselves.

If you struggle with assertiveness you're not alone, it's something a lot of people find difficult. It doesn't mean you're weak or there's something wrong with you. Sometimes it's just that assertiveness isn't something we're really taught, not directly anyway. And if those around us aren't assertive either, we don't get to pick up those skills through the usual channels, like watching and learning from our parents. A lot of people shy away from speaking up because they feel they're meant to quietly follow some unwritten rule, this belief that you should never speak your mind. But that's not right, and of course you should speak up for yourself. The good news is, assertiveness is a skill that you can teach yourself. With practice, it can become something very natural, and you can feel confident in it. That's what we'll do in this chapter. Let's get started!

Chapter 1:
What Is Assertiveness?

Assertiveness is a communication skill that helps you speak up for yourself directly, honestly and respectfully, without being passive, aggressive or even passive-aggressive. Assertiveness is about standing up for yourself like an advocate who knows their needs matter, because you recognize you have value. As a psychologist, I would say it's one of the most fundamental life skills alongside boundaries – with which it has a close connection. Assertiveness is a communication tool you use to express your boundaries to other people. And both assertiveness and boundaries work together to help you have balanced and respectful interactions and relationships. The difference, though, between boundaries and assertiveness is that boundaries apply to your interactions with others and to personal limits you set for yourself – like your time, work, rest and personal space. Assertiveness, on the other hand, is a skill you use only when directed towards others.

Being assertive helps you get your needs met, achieve your goals, feel good about yourself; it makes you happier, helps you feel safe, and creates an environment where you feel calmer and in control. It builds your confidence and helps you value your worth. It also improves your communication skills and makes you better at facing conflict and disagreement. Which means you have fewer unresolved issues, which means fewer resentments beneath the surface. Assertiveness helps align what you're feeling on the inside with your expressions on the outside, and that's why it reduces that resentment-related stress. Because you're no longer pretending to think or feel something that, deep down, feels completely opposite to your truth.

The positive impact of assertiveness on mental health and emotional well-being is well known. Research shows that being more assertive can reduce stress, anxiety, social anxiety and depression, improve self-expression and communication skills, boost self-esteem and enhance emotional resilience.[17] It's also known to help people regulate their emotions – which is the ability to manage your emotions in stressful situations so you react in balanced and healthy ways. All in all, it's a massive boost to your well-being and can enhance the quality of your life by helping you feel more confident in speaking up for yourself.[18]

Chapter 2:
Why Does Being Assertive Feel So Hard?

For some people, it goes back to past experiences. Maybe you tried to be assertive once, and it didn't land well. Maybe it caused conflict, or felt like it backfired. And that kind of experience can linger in your mind, influencing how you act later. It can also be shaped by how you were raised, and the social conditioning that encouraged you to be easy-going, agreeable, not make a fuss. You might have received cultural or social messages that say being assertive is selfish, or wrong, or somehow goes against being a 'good' or selfless person. Another barrier can be fear. That quiet worry that if you speak up, it'll upset someone, or shift how they see you in a way you can't control and don't like. Or perhaps people see you as selfless and caring, which can feel rewarding – and you don't want to risk losing that by being assertive. So you hold back. But that can trap you in a role that others find likeable, while you start to lose a part of yourself. Another obstacle is overthinking being assertive, second-guessing yourself or questioning whether you even have the right to be. You might be in the habit of prioritizing other people's needs. Especially if you tend to people-please, the idea of assertiveness can feel like it clashes with that. Or maybe you've misunderstood what assertiveness actually is. Perhaps it's been confused with rudeness, bluntness or aggression, so you steer clear of it. Sometimes the barrier is not knowing what you need or feel in the moment. And when you don't know that, it's nearly impossible to put those needs into words, let alone express them out loud. Or it might be as simple (and as real) as this: no one ever taught you how to be assertive. It's not something most of us are born knowing. For many people, it's a skill that has to be learned. And if you didn't get the chance, it makes sense that it would feel challenging. Assertiveness is worth learning because without it, it's easy to be overlooked, taken advantage of or pulled into other people's demands in ways that don't feel fair or respectful.

Chapter 3:
How to Be Assertive

In this section I'll show you step by step how to become assertive, with practical skills that you can apply right away.

1. Know the needs you want to assert

Assertiveness is all about communicating the needs you want to assert, and the first step is to really understand what those needs are. It might seem like it's obvious, but knowing your own needs in these situations isn't automatic for everyone. So, here's a simple exercise to help you start tuning into those needs, so you can move from just feeling something to actually expressing it in a way that feels clear and assertive. Think back to past situations where you wished you'd spoken up but didn't. What did you need in that moment? What do you wish you'd said?

Looking back like this helps you see where your needs went unspoken and gives you a clearer idea of what you were wanting at the time. You can apply this to more recent situations, too. And if you want a more structured way to practise building your assertiveness, you can also make it a daily/weekly habit to identify at least one situation where you wanted to be assertive but didn't quite get there. Write down the same things: what you needed and what you wish you'd said.

You'll start noticing patterns – whether it's when you're in certain situations or with particular people – where being assertive feels hard. You'll also start seeing common threads in what you needed or wanted to express. Once you see those patterns, think about how you could tweak what you wished you'd said so it feels easier and more natural – something you could use if a similar situation came up again.

The key is to make sure the words you choose feel comfortable enough that you could actually say them out loud. For example, if you wished you'd said, 'No way am I taking on extra work, so cheeky,' you could refine this unassertive phrase into a more assertive and manageable one like, 'I'd love to help, but I'm at my limit and can't take more on right now.' This refining process is about bridging the gap between what you might feel like saying and what you feel is appropriate to express assertively, while also remembering that being assertive isn't rude or aggressive; it's about effective communication. Coming up with phrases like these helps prepare you for the future. When you keep using this skill, over time you'll build a bank of phrases that are ready to go for whenever you need them.

2. Ready-to-use phrases for everyday life

Now, let's look at a wider range of assertiveness phrases to help you get more used to the feel of this kind of language. The more familiar it becomes, the easier it is to reach for when you need it. I've included a range of phrases with some common situations where they might come up. But you don't need to use them exactly as they are, or in the same situations. Think of them as your starting points, then you can tweak them, make them your own and shape them to fit how you speak and whatever moment you're in.

You might read some of these phrases and feel a twinge

of discomfort. You might even cringe at a few – and that's completely normal. It doesn't mean assertiveness isn't for you. Often, it's exactly in that discomfort that growth begins. New things, especially those involving other people, can feel awkward at first. It's like walking in shoes that haven't been broken in yet, they feel stiff and unfamiliar to start with. But being comfortable with assertiveness isn't about waiting for the unease to disappear. It's about letting the discomfort be there and doing it anyway. Confidence doesn't come first, it grows from the doing. So if something feels a bit strange, that's not a warning sign, it's proof you're stepping into the right space. Step by step, that initial stiffness softens and what once felt difficult starts to feel more natural.

When you just want to say no

Saying no can be tough for many people. It seems like such a simple word, in fact, probably one of the first we learn as toddlers, and we say it a lot in those early years. But as we grow and go through experiences that shape us, that simple word becomes tangled with fears of disappointing others, of conflict and general anxiety. Sometimes, we need to return to the comfort we had in those early years, when saying no came naturally, without second-guessing ourselves. Because at its core, saying no is a way of respecting yourself. Your needs, your time, energy and your mental well-being. So here are some ways to say it:

'No.'

'No, thank you.'

'I'm not comfortable with that.'

'I'd prefer not to.'

'No, I can't do that.'

If you do want to give a reason when you're saying no, here are a few ways you can do that with a simple, clear explanation. Depending on the situation, and who you're talking to, you might choose to add a sorry. But only if you genuinely mean it. Try not to use it as a way to patch over any guilt that might come up, because you don't need to apologize for setting your limits.

> 'I can't chat tonight, I've got some things I need to get done.'
>
> 'I can't do lunch today, I've got a lot of work to get through.'
>
> 'Sorry, I can't do today, how about we do next week?'
>
> 'I can't stay late today, I've got plans.'

When someone asks you to do something but you can't or don't want to

> 'Sorry, I can't help with that.'
>
> 'Thank you, but I won't be able to do that.'
>
> 'I appreciate you thinking of me, but I can't take that on right now.'

When someone is rude to you

> 'I won't be spoken to like that.'
>
> 'Please don't speak to me like that.'
>
> 'Please speak respectfully to me.'

When someone interrupts you

> 'Please listen to me without interrupting.'

'Please let me finish.'

'Please hold on for a minute while I finish speaking.'

When you want to express a different opinion

'I see it differently, my perspective is . . .'

'That's not accurate, let me explain.'

'I accept your opinion; my view is . . .'

When your perspective is questioned

'When there are multiple people, there are multiple truths.'

'You might not believe it, but it is my truth.'

'I respect that that is your truth, but mine is different.'

'From your perspective, I'm sure you're right.'

'What did you hear me say?'

When someone's behaviour makes you uncomfortable

'I'm not comfortable with your behaviour, please stop.'

'Please don't do that.'

'If you don't stop, I will have to leave.'

When your words are misinterpreted

'There's been a misunderstanding, I said . . .'

'Let me clarify, what I meant was . . .'

'You've misunderstood me, that's not how it is, it's . . .'

When someone asks to borrow money/material items

'I don't lend things out, I never have.'

'I can't, that's not something I'm comfortable lending.'

When you want a refund

'I'd like to return this for a refund, please.'

When you're unhappy with food or service you've received

'I'm not happy with this meal because . . . [e.g., it's cold, it has a hair in it, etc.]. Please can I get a replacement?'

'I'm not satisfied with the service I've received because . . .'

'There's been a mistake, please can you help resolve it.'

When someone is pressuring you or being persistent

'I've already made my decision.'

'I've said no, and I'm not going to change my mind.'

'I'm not interested in talking more about it, please respect that.'

When your personal information is shared without consent

'Please don't talk about me without my permission.'

'I would have preferred that you kept that between us.'

'I'm not comfortable with you talking about me, please don't do it again.'

When someone comments on your appearance

'Please don't comment on my body/appearance.'

'I'm not comfortable with comments about my looks.'

If any of these phrases stand out to you, and you've got a feeling you might need them one day, it's worth spending some time with them before that day comes, especially if they feel uncomfortable. One simple way to do that is to say these phrases out loud now and then. While you're making dinner, walking to the shops, sitting in traffic, standing in the shower. You can even try saying them to yourself in the mirror. And yes, it might feel awkward or even a bit cringe at first. But there's something powerful about hearing your own voice say the things you're usually scared to say, while seeing yourself do so. It takes the sharpness out of the words and makes them feel more natural. If you've got someone in your life you trust, you could try saying a few of them out loud to them too, just to get used to the sound and feel of them in conversation. When the real moment arrives, when someone crosses a line, or you feel like speaking up for your needs, you won't be scrambling for what to say. You'll already have the words sitting on the tip of your tongue. Not because you rehearsed a script, but because they've become part of your language. Something you can easily reach for when you need it most.

3. Build your confidence layer by layer

Our next skill is all about slowly building your assertiveness skills. If it feels tough to be assertive, try starting with small steps and just keep practising until it becomes more natural. Once you've done one thing, move on to the next, then the next, increasing the challenge a little each time. Over time, as your confidence builds, you'll start to notice you're naturally more assertive in different parts of your life. It's like trying anything else new, at first things feel shaky, but little by little, you start to feel more solid. I've put together a sample hierarchy to give you an idea of how to approach this kind of skill-building, starting with easier situations and working up to the harder ones as your confidence grows. Doing it this way can make it feel a lot more manageable. You'll have the easier ones in your pocket first, then when you take on the tougher ones, it won't feel as intimidating. This list is just a suggestion, though. You don't have to follow it exactly. Maybe you'd rather just tackle things as they come up, that's totally fine too. The point of the list is to see how you can start small and build up, at your own pace if you need to. The order might not necessarily be easiest-to-hardest for you; what feels easy to one person can be more challenging for another, and vice versa. So use these ideas to find what works best for you.

Stage 1 – The foundation: starting small and simple

Saying no to an invitation or offer.

Making a phone call to enquire about something.

Booking or changing an appointment.

Asking for clarification when you don't understand.

Asking for help.

Asking where something is, in a shop for example.

Ordering food or drinks in a cafe/restaurant.

Stage 2 – Stepping up to address common everyday situations

Querying a billing issue.

Asking for a refund or exchange.

Expressing dissatisfaction with food or drink in a cafe/restaurant.

Expressing dissatisfaction with a product or service.

Telling someone their behaviour is making you uncomfortable.

Turning down extra responsibility.

Correcting someone when they make an assumption about you that is inaccurate.

Stage 3 – Increasing assertiveness

Expressing boundaries about your personal space.

Voicing your opinion in a group discussion.

Asking someone to stop interrupting you.

Refusing to lend money or material possessions.

Telling someone their behaviour makes you uncomfortable.

Dealing with interruptions.

Stage 4 – Advancing your assertiveness

Just saying no.

Speaking up to inappropriate comments or behaviours.

Dealing with disagreements in a professional or personal relationship.

Continuing to practise assertive skills in everyday life.

4. Use the broken record technique

The broken record technique is a simple, effective way to be assertive. You calmly repeat your point until it's heard. It's so effective that it's used by all kinds of people – parents, teachers, managers, salespeople and even negotiators. Repeating your point calmly shows the other person that you mean what you say, and you're standing your ground. When someone isn't listening, there's no need to change your words or try to convince them in another way. You can just keep re-stating your point. Let them talk if they want to, then gently go back to repeating your message. Keep your tone calm, and your body relaxed, your goal is to stay steady. When you repeat yourself, make sure your words are short and simple too. That way, they're easy to say again and again. Avoid adding new details, because it opens the door for debate. Stick to your original point and it'll be harder for them to divert you. If they're not getting it you can say something like, 'As I was saying . . .' and then repeat your point. If they comment on your repetition, you can respond with something like, 'Yes, because this is important to me,' and then again re-state what you've said. It might seem like it'll drag on forever, but it actually won't. A few repetitions is usually enough before the other person gets the message. Give it a try – holding your position like this will help you feel more confident and in control. Here's a quick example of how this technique works:

> *You*: I'd like a refund, please.
> *Shop Assistant*: Can we offer you an exchange, or a voucher instead?
> *You*: No, thanks, I'd like a refund, please.

Shop Assistant: Do you know the voucher is actually valid for a whole year, and you can use it on anything in the store?
You: I'd like a refund, please.
Shop Assistant: Most people are happy with the voucher. Are you sure?
You: Yes, I'd like a refund, please.

5. Embrace compliments assertively

Being assertive is about expressing and claiming what's true for you, and that includes receiving compliments confidently. When you accept a compliment, you're saying to yourself, 'Yes, that's true about me and I accept it.' Doing so helps you practise the same mindset you use when stating your needs. It's about claiming your value, staying grounded and responding with confidence. Receiving compliments also reinforces your sense of worth, enhancing your ability to act assertively in other areas of your life. It's a small, low-stakes way to work on the mindset and skills that assertiveness relies on. A lot of people find it hard though, not because they don't like and appreciate the kind words, but because a compliment can land right where it feels uncomfortable. It creates this tension between the good someone else sees in you, and the doubts you hold onto inside about yourself. And that clash can feel awkward. So maybe you brush it aside, laugh it off, change the subject, or make a joke about yourself to take the attention off you. You might also quietly question if they really meant it – because in a strange way, it feels safer to doubt it than to actually let it in. It can feel more comfortable than the vulnerability of being seen in a good light, not because you don't want to be seen that way, but because it doesn't match how you see yourself. And that mismatch can feel uncomfortable. You might also worry that accepting compliments might make you appear arrogant, like you're full of yourself. But pride is usually not the problem. It's the discomfort underneath, the part of you that still isn't sure you should feel good about yourself. Rejecting compliments is like refusing a gift that you really want but say no to. And when you keep doing this, it reinforces your belief that you don't deserve good things, that you shouldn't feel good, and that you shouldn't believe that you're good. Accepting compliments assertively is a step towards feeling more secure in yourself. It's not arrogance, it just means you're letting something kind in. So, the next time someone gives you a compliment, even if it feels a little awkward, try to accept it. Look them in the eye, smile, and try saying one of these:

> 'Thank you.'
>
> 'That's so kind of you, thank you.'
>
> 'You've really made my day with that, thank you!'
>
> 'Thank you, I've put a lot of effort into this, so I'm really happy to hear that.'
>
> 'Thank you, I've worked really hard on that.'

A handy reference for assertiveness

I've walked you through five different skills to help you build your assertiveness, covering all sorts of situations and a range of tools. Before we wrap up this chapter, I'm going to give you a simple and handy reference guide with some key principles of assertiveness. Think of this as your final ingredient to really lock in what assertiveness is (and isn't). It includes pointers about body language, along with dos and don'ts.

Assertiveness is respectful, clear and direct

It's not about being aggressive, so try to avoid sarcasm, a condescending tone, being abrupt, shouting, blaming or using putdowns and offensive words. These kinds of behaviours can come across as attacking, even if that's not your intent. And when that happens, it's harder for other people to really hear what you're saying. Your goal is to stay clear, without creating tension.

Be conscious of your body language

Make sure your body language supports what you're saying and how you want to come across. Have good eye contact, avoid standing too close or invading someone's personal space, and keep your body open and relaxed. Try not to cross your arms, it can signal discomfort or defensiveness. Don't use intimidating gestures or expressions – like pointing, clenching your fists, or towering over others. These actions can come across as passive-aggressive or even aggressive, and that can make it harder for your message to land the way you want it to.

The way you speak is crucial. Speak with a calm, steady and relaxed tone of voice. It helps you come across as confident, and it also sets the tone for the conversation – keeping things calm. Keep your volume somewhere in the middle, not too loud and not too quiet. And remember, calm doesn't mean cold. You can still sound warm, friendly, even caring, while being assertive. Keep your phrases simple and fluent, without too much hesitation. Try not to ramble or circle around the point – just say what you need to say and then stop. Over-explaining can water down your message. You don't need to fill every silence, a pause can be part of your message too.

Don't undermine your confidence by how you speak

Try not to let your words sound like a question by adding a rising intonation at the end of a sentence. Instead, speak with a clear, steady tone, and think of each phrase as having an audible full stop at the end. This means saying what you need to say, then pausing. That space is there for you to take a breath, for the other person to take in what you've said and respond – so just let it be.

Don't apologize unnecessarily. Question whether you actually need to use the word 'sorry'. Try to avoid apologizing too often or out of habit, there's no need for excessive or repeated apologies. 'Sorry' has its place – like when believe you've done something wrong or if you feel regret about something. But when it's used too much, or unnecessarily, it can undermine your message and your confidence. So save it for when you mean it.

Don't use phrases that convey insecurity

These kinds of phrases can weaken your message by creating uncertainty and self-doubt. They can downplay your needs and make the other person think what you're saying isn't that important.

Here are some examples:

> 'Well, if you ask me, I think . . .'
>
> 'If it's not too much trouble . . .'
>
> 'It probably doesn't matter . . .'

Things to hold onto . . .

Assertiveness is a core communication skill that can really shape how you show up with others. It's about finding your voice and using it to speak up for yourself in a way that's respectful and honest.

Being assertive means standing up for your needs because you recognize your value. It's about becoming your own advocate, knowing that what you think, feel and need matters.

There are lots of reasons it can feel hard to be assertive. Maybe it's anxiety, a dip in confidence, the way you were brought up, what you learned about speaking up, or just not knowing how to start.

Assertiveness is something you can build, step by step. It starts with getting clear on the needs you want to assert, saying the things you need to say, learning to say no and preparing for the moments that usually trip you up.

Part Six

How You Stop People-Pleasing

'I reply to messages as soon as I get them,' Brett told me. 'I feel like I have to, you know? They might think I'm upset with them if I take too long. If someone says let's do this or that, I just go with it, even if I don't really want to.'

'I'm always on alert, wondering if someone's thirsty, hungry, or not feeling well. I can't relax or sit still when I'm with my friends or family; I feel this urge to keep doing things for them, even if they haven't asked. If they even mention being sick, I'm on it – getting them painkillers, water, a blanket, whatever will help,' Natasha told me.

'I'll lend them anything, even when I know I might not get it back. I've done it so many times,' Nazia told me. 'Sometimes, I'll give away things I love, like my trainers or a jumper, just because they said they like it. I feel this overwhelming need to give people things. I'll spend money on them without thinking, even when I'm struggling myself. If someone asks for a favour, I'm there. I'll cancel plans and push through my tiredness so I can help them.'

And Molly explained, 'I step in when the conversation goes silent because I don't want anyone to feel awkward. If someone interrupts someone else, it sticks with me. I'll wait until they're done, and then I'll ask the person who got interrupted what they were saying. I just want to make sure no one feels left out or ignored. If it looks like someone's on the outside, I try to give them extra attention. I always notice those things; it's like I have a radar for them.'

These examples might seem very specific, but what they all have in common is they put other people's needs above your own. They also show the wide spectrum of people-pleasing, and how it shows up in communication, physical caretaking, financial or material giving, and social or emotional smoothing. And the causes span just as wide: fear of disapproval or conflict, feeling overly responsible for other people's comfort, trying to earn love or acceptance through sacrifice, or constantly managing social dynamics so no one feels uneasy. The price you pay for constantly bending over backward, putting everyone else's needs first while ignoring your own, can be steep. The thing about being a people-pleaser is that it doesn't just make you do one of these things. It's like a blanket of behaviours that covers so many parts of your life. It can become what you're about.

I'm certain that you can see at least one piece of yourself in these stories. Maybe you've caught yourself doing something similar, without even realizing the toll it takes on you. In this part of the book, we'll look at why you became a people-pleaser in the first place, the hidden costs of being this way, and – most importantly – how you can start letting go of it, step by step. The goal is to help you build a healthier, more balanced life where you can give to others without losing yourself in the process.

Chapter 1:
What Is People-Pleasing?

People-pleasing is when you put other people's needs or opinions before your own. You do this because you're afraid of disappointing others, of being disliked, rejected, or being seen as difficult, or because you feel like you're not enough unless you're constantly doing things for others. But the thing is, by doing that, you end up reinforcing the very belief you're trying to run from – that you aren't enough unless you're constantly proving your worth. People-pleasing can show up in all areas of life, at work, at home, in relationships and in friendships. It makes you try hard to make others happy, even when it leaves you feeling drained. You're probably the one who remembers everyone's preferences, makes sure everyone else is comfortable, and you read the room like it's second nature, but no one really notices when you're the one who's quietly running on empty. You say yes to things you don't really want to do. It feels like your role is to surrender to the comfort, opinions or needs of others. And, it's dangerous not just because people can end up taking advantage of you, but because that voice inside you, the one that knows what you want, fades away.

You're known as reliable, helpful, kind and always there. You tell people what they want to hear, rarely express criticism and avoid disagreement. It makes you easy to be around, but hard to truly know. Others think the version they see is the real you, but it isn't, because of everything you have to hide for their benefit. You're also a serial apologist, saying sorry for no good reason over and over again. You believe self-sacrifice is the way to keep others close so they like you, need you and think positively of you. You're great at telling people exactly what they want to hear. Not only does it please them, but it also helps you avoid conflict. You're a brilliant facilitator, making sure everyone else feels heard and seen, but rarely feel like you can share your own thoughts or feelings without worrying you'll upset someone. You hardly ever advocate for your own needs, and you don't have clear boundaries. You avoid setting limits because you think other people won't like them.

I can almost hear you thinking, 'People-pleasing sounds quite dark, when actually, isn't it a good thing to help people?' And yes, helping others is definitely a good thing, but that help has to be healthy. Healthy helping doesn't come at the cost of your own well-being; it's not about you walking around carrying everyone else's weight while your own well-being takes a hit. Research shows it's all about finding a balance that ensures you're not overwhelmed by the demands of helping.[19] Overdoing it to the point of exhaustion can cancel out any positive effects. Healthy help is a balance of genuine care, willingness and the ability to care for yourself at the same time.

Where does your people-pleasing show up?

I've set out three questions on the next page to help you see the specific situations, people or contexts that trigger people-pleasing in you. Understanding these patterns is a first step towards making changes, it gives you a clear picture of where to focus your efforts. I'd like you to come back to what you've noted down from these questions later, once you've learned the skills to help you move away from people-pleasing. As you go through the questions, you'll probably notice patterns, whether it's particular situations, triggers or certain people that cause you to people-please.

1. What areas of your life do you notice people-pleasing behaviours showing up the most? Is it with everyone, family, friends, work, relationships? Any other situation?

2. In these areas, what triggers the strongest urge to people-please? Is it to get approval, to feel loved, to avoid conflict, or another reason? If so, what is it?

3. Do you tend to people-please everyone, or does it happen more with certain people? If so, who are they?

Chapter 2:
Why You're a People-Pleaser

I've already mentioned how people-pleasing can come from fears of conflict or rejection, or from wanting closeness, approval and validation. These are the surface-level reasons, and they can stand on their own. But sometimes, they go deeper, with roots in your past, or personality traits, trauma, learned behaviours, a fear of being authentic, anxiety, or maybe something else. Whatever the cause, understanding where your people-pleasing patterns come from can really help you see why you do what you do, and what keeps driving it. This awareness won't change the past or undo what shaped your people-pleasing, but it does give you the power to recognize what's happening and why, so you can choose to respond in a different way. When you catch yourself slipping into people-pleasing, you can pause and remind yourself: 'This is an old pattern, an old influence. I don't have to act from that place any more.' That's the magic of awareness – it gives you the ability to choose your reaction, rather than just letting old habits call the shots. As you go through this chapter, pay attention to the different causes of people-pleasing that resonate with you, and use that insight to better understand your situation.

1. Personality traits

Agreeableness, high empathy, conscientiousness and perfectionistic traits can all make you more prone to people-pleasing. But having these traits doesn't automatically mean you'll become a people-pleaser – the behaviour is more complex than a straight cause-and-effect. These traits can also have really positive effects in relationships. They help you connect, care and show up for others. But in the context of people-pleasing, that same warmth can tip into something that goes against you. In the sections below, I'll break down how each of these seemingly positive traits can slip into unhealthy people-pleasing, and show you the toll that can take on your well-being.

Agreeableness: this trait means you have a desire for peace and harmony, and when you have that, of course you want to prioritize other people's needs. It can look like agreeing with others even when you actually disagree. You smooth things over, hold your tongue, offer what looks like an easy yes, all to keep things calm. Even if it means suppressing your own opinion and needs. You want to avoid conflict and keep everything nice and positive in interactions and relationships.

Empathy: if you're high in empathy you'll deeply internalize other people's emotions, so much so that it feels like you're carrying their feelings. And it's coupled with a strong urge to help the person who is struggling, even if that person doesn't want your help and isn't engaged in solving their own problems. You're an all-in fixer, or rescuer, even when it's one-sided. And because you become so consumed by other people's feelings and problems, it means your own get neglected, quietly piling up in the background, waiting for you to turn around and notice them too.

Conscientiousness: this trait is when you have a strong sense of responsibility and the weight often lands heavy. It can make it difficult for you to say no because you're anxious about letting others down. You feel a pressure to meet expectations, which can mean you overcommit and prioritize outside demands over your own needs, and you will do this even if you're already overwhelmed.

Perfectionism: This trait, although seen as something positive and polished, often praised because it looks impressive, hides a deep pressure underneath. It's commonly rooted in insecurity and the need to appear competent and avoid judgement at all costs. It can drive you to meet every expectation, while maintaining a facade of perfection and control. It means that you take on too much, and you hide your struggles in order to appear flawless. You present a version of yourself that looks seamless on the outside, even while things are fraying on the inside. You hold yourself to very high standards, making it hard to say no. And you rarely admit you have any limitations; it's go go go, like running on a treadmill that never stops.

2. Trauma

People-pleasing can also be a trauma response shaped by experiences of rejection, abandonment, disapproval, neglect or even abuse. If you grew up in an environment where making others happy was key to your survival, it makes sense that it became second nature. As a child, you might have learned that keeping your caregivers (or others) happy was the only way to get your needs met and feel safe, whether emotionally or physically. So, you adapted. You may also have started people-pleasing to avoid conflict or punishment, or to prevent yourself from being ignored. Over time, your people-pleasing became automatic, your brain's way of keeping you safe or getting the outcome you need. Even long after those experiences have passed, the patterns you learned can stick with you, making people-pleasing feel like an automatic reflex rather than a conscious choice. Many people who have experienced trauma find themselves enjoying taking care of others because it helps heal the part of them that needed care. In doing so, they get to experience the feeling of care, even if it's not directed at them.

All these patterns of thinking and behaving can feel like they're still helping you now because they once did. But as an adult, these people-pleasing habits don't help you; they keep you stuck in a cycle of sacrificing your own needs for survival. You'll still survive, even if you stop people-pleasing, but if you don't stop, it can cause you more pain and suffering. The very thing that helped you survive a trauma – people-pleasing – now has the potential to become the source of new pain in your life.

3. Learned behaviour

People-pleasing can also be a learned behaviour. You see others engaging in people-pleasing behaviours, you witness positive outcomes (like approval or praise), and then you do the same thing yourself. Witnessing these positive reactions naturally makes you think, 'This is how I should be.' Early on in your life, you might have also seen people-pleasing behaviour in the people who matter most to you, like your parents or caregivers. As children, we believe their way is the right way, they're our first teachers. So it makes sense that you'd pick up on those behaviours and start acting in the same ways. Growing up, you might have also been taught that putting others first makes you a good person. A lot of parents encourage their children to always help others, which is a great lesson. But sometimes they don't explain where the boundaries around that help lie. That might be because they haven't figured out those boundaries themselves.

4. Fear of Authenticity

Like many people-pleasers you probably fear showing who you really are. Because deep down, you believe that if people saw and knew the real you, including what you actually think and feel – they wouldn't like you. Worse than that, they might even hate you, or stop talking to you altogether. Being your authentic self isn't just about allowing your flaws to show (which we all have). It's also about voicing your opinions, needs and boundaries, even when that feels uncomfrotable. This might mean saying no when you want to, speaking up when you disagree with something, or admitting you're not okay instead of hiding how you feel. But because this feels so risky, you make yourself agreeable and accommodating, and continue making everything easy for everyone else. People-pleasing is like your armour, it's a way for you to protect those vulnerable parts of you, that feel too fragile to be seen.

5. Anxiety

Anxiety can also fuel people-pleasing. And, it generally comes from the fear of being judged, disliked or worrying that you're not 'good enough.' It can create a constant undercurrent of fear, the fear of losing friends, relationships or facing rejection.

It's that gnawing feeling of uncertainty about how people *could* react to you. It's all the unknowns that your mind runs through, trying to figure out every possible 'what-if' that could happen. So people-pleasing kicks in, trying to stop those what-ifs from becoming reality. Common 'what-ifs' are:

What if I bore them?

What if I annoy them?

What if they don't like me?

What if they don't like what I say?

What if I don't do enough for them?

Your mind will try to prepare for the worst-case scenario, thinking that if you have a plan for each what-if, at least you'll be ready. So, let's say if one of those 'what-ifs' is: 'What if they stop liking me?' you'll do everything you can to make sure they don't. Or maybe you think: 'What if I said something wrong?' And after that, you start holding back, you become quieter or agree more with others, even when deep down, you actually don't. You basically stop saying what you really think, just to stay on the safe side. By doing this, you might feel like you have some control over how others see you, and how they react to you. It can feel like a way to avoid the reactions you're most afraid of.

Beyond just trying to manage all the 'what-ifs,' people-pleasing can also bring some relief to an anxious mind. When you people-please and others respond with warmth, when they seem to like you or appreciate you, it gives you a sense of being wanted, valued or accepted. In those moments, your anxiety can ease a little.

Chapter 3:
The Price You Pay for People-Pleasing

When people-pleasing is a long-term pattern, it can take a real toll on you, affecting your physical and mental well-being. You might be missing out on sleep, exercise, hobbies, skipping meals or meaningful time with others. In my clinical work, I've seen a direct link between persistent people-pleasing and mental health problems, such as anxiety, depression, low self-esteem, trauma and more. People-pleasing teaches you that your needs don't matter, or at least, not as much as everyone else's. Over time, that message can sink deep. And when it does, it chips away at your sense of worth. When you keep putting others first, that inner sense of value starts to wear thin. And as your self-worth fades, the fear of rejection or being left alone can grow bigger. So you people-please even more to earn approval, convinced you need to try harder now, since deep down you feel worth even less.

People-pleasing can also drain your energy and motivation, leaving little for taking care of yourself, pursuing your own goals, or just getting through your day without undue stress. When you're constantly focused on other people's needs, you end up neglecting the very things that would stop you from burning out. When you keep putting everyone else first, your own needs can get buried so deeply that you forget what they even are. You might wake up one day and wonder, 'Why didn't I think about this? Why didn't I take care of that?' When you lose touch with your own needs, it's also hard to know where your boundaries are. And without those limits, you can't protect yourself from being taken advantage of, and you can easily end up stuck in situations that aren't good for you.

Ironically, the very thing you're doing to feel accepted and loved – the people-pleasing – ends up reinforcing the idea that you're only worthy when you're giving. When you keep showing up for others, over and over, without receiving that same care or consideration in return, it takes a further toll. You might feel used, resentful, still unsure of your worth, but now carrying these frustrations on top of that too. And longer term, it's just not sustainable. You're pouring from a cup that hasn't been refilled in a long time. And when you keep going like this, eventually, you reach a point where there's not much left, and you feel totally depleted.

We often assume the cost of people-pleasing is only mental or emotional, but it can affect you physically too. Research has looked at self-silencing, something people-pleasers often do, which means suppressing your own thoughts, needs, feelings, or opinions to avoid disapproval or keep things peaceful. It's been found to affect both men and women.[20] Self-silencing has been linked to worse mental health, and even physical health issues.[21]

Understanding the many costs of people-pleasing can be a powerful motivator, because it shows you exactly how this behaviour harms you, or could harm you if it continues. So take a moment to reflect on the costs you see in your own life, and let that awareness drive you towards breaking free from these patterns.

Chapter 4:
How to Stop Being a People-Pleaser

In this chapter, we'll look at how you can start to move away from people-pleasing. First, we'll explore how your values can help guide you, so instead of just reacting, you're making choices based on what matters most to you. Then we'll look at how you can do things differently in the moments when people-pleasing shows up. We'll also look at how to work through the guilt that might surface when you begin setting boundaries. And finally we'll explore how to handle the self-critical thoughts that often tag along.

1. Use your values to stop people-pleasing

The urge to people-please can feel automatic, especially if you've been doing it for a long time. It becomes second nature. To start to change that pattern you need something steady to anchor you, and that's where your values come in. People-pleasing often pulls you away from what really matters to you. It steers you towards choices based on what you think others want, or how you want to be seen, instead of what you truly value. Over time it can start to shape your life into something that doesn't quite feel like your own. People-pleasing becomes the default setting, while your inner compass, the voice of your values, is pointing you somewhere else, but you're not really listening. When you pause and reconnect with that compass, and really look at the direction it's pointing in, you can start to make choices that feel more like you. Decisions that come from your values, not just the pull to please. And that can really start to shift how you respond in those people-pleasing moments.

So how do you actually begin to put this into practice? Start by looking back at your list of values (see pp. 43–4). Let those values be your guide on how you want to respond to those triggers. Reflect on the kind of person you want to be and the life you want to live, even when people-pleasing triggers show up.

One way to use this skill is to think back on a few past experiences, recent or old, where you fell into people-pleasing. Then, take a value and ask yourself questions like these:

> 'If I had acted in line with this value, even with my people-pleasing habits, what might I have done differently?'
>
> 'What choice can I make that reflects this value?'
>
> 'What small step can I take here to make sure my actions line up with my values?'

Do this for each value on your list, to uncover actions that will move you towards what really matters. It will give you a clearer picture of the kinds of choices you'd rather make next time. Be sure to write these down or keep a mental note of them, so you've got something to come back to the next time a people-pleasing trigger shows up. And if you've already done the first task in this part of the book on p. 141, you'll have a list of your common people-pleasing triggers. Alongside that, you're now building a ready-to-go guide of values-based actions. It's all about getting clearer on what you want to do, not just what feels expected. Here are a few worked examples to show how using values-based action might look in everyday life.

The value of honesty

The value of honesty is about retutning to your own inner truth. It's about being truthful and sincere, expressing your genuine thoughts and feelings, and acting in accordance with them. When a people-pleasing trigger shows up, ask yourself:

> 'What do I actually think or feel about this?'
>
> 'What would I say or do if I were being honest?'
>
> 'Even if I feel uncomfortable, what action would be most in line with what's true for me?'

Example response: 'My honest answer is I don't really agree with what they're asking. So, I don't actually want to do it. If I were being honest, I might say something like: "I don't agree with that, so I won't be able to help you with it." But it feels hard to say that, especially because I'm used to saying yes. If I want to uphold my value of honesty, even when I feel anxious about how it might land, I could say: "I'm really sorry, I can't do that. I hope it works out." It doesn't have to be dramatic. It just has to have my truth in it.'

The value of patience

The value of patience is about allowing space, accepting delay, giving yourself time, and meeting situations with balance instead of reacting on impulse. This helps stop split-second reactions that come out of fear or habit. When that familiar urge to act quickly and please others shows up, it can really help to pause and ask yourself:

'What would I actually do here if I were practising patience?'

'How might I respond if I gave myself just a bit more time?'

'What would a more measured, thoughtful choice look like in this moment?'

Example response: 'If I were making a decision based on my value of patience, I wouldn't actually give them an answer straight away. I'd give myself a bit more time to think about what I actually want to do, what's good or bad about it. This time will also help me look at my values and make sure I make a thoughtful decision. So I could just say to them, "Let me check and get back to you." So I have the time I need.'

The value of personal well-being

The value of personal well-being is about looking after yourself and caring for your health, happiness and emotional needs. Living by this value means checking in with yourself, especially when you feel that pull to put others first. To do that you can ask yourself:

'How will saying yes to this situation affect my well-being?'

'How will saying no to this situation affect my well-being?'

Example response: 'Saying yes to this means I'll have a very late night. I'm sleep-deprived with all the stress of work this week; I haven't slept very well. Saying no to this will mean that I can have a relaxing evening and try to catch up on some sleep. I can express my decision based on this value by saying to them, "I'm so burnt out from work this week and the lack of sleep, so sorry, I can't make it. Hopefully, there'll be another time."'

The value of harmony

The value of harmony is about cultivating a sense of calm, peace and balance in your life, and understanding that people-pleasing doesn't bring true harmony. Both within yourself and in your relationships. To honour this value you need to focus on choices that support this harmony. To do that you can ask yourself:

> 'Will the action I'm considering bring me peace and harmony, or disturb it?'
>
> 'What choice could bring the most harmony?'
>
> 'What do I need to say or do to protect that harmony?'

Example response: 'They asked me to phone their boyfriend for them, to try and sort out the problems they were having, and I considered it – but honestly, that's not going to bring me harmony; it'll bring me anxiety and stress. I already feel super anxious just thinking about it. It doesn't feel healthy to get involved like that. The choice that brings me the most harmony is to tell them, "I can't do it. I feel so stressed and uncomfortable about it. I really hope things work out for you."'

2. How to respond differently in people-pleasing moments

When you've been people-pleasing for a long time, it can start to feel like second nature. You find yourself saying yes or going along with things without really stopping to think about what you actually want. This section is about helping you recognize those moments so you can respond differently, acting from a place of intention rather than the same default pattern. In this section, you'll get some simple phrases to use in the moments when people-pleasing triggers present. These are alternatives to your automatic yes or quick agreement, they're simple things you can say that create space for you to respond more intentionally. You can use these phrases as they are, or tweak them to sound more like you. It can help to memorize one or two, so they come to mind more easily in those moments when it's hard to think clearly on the spot.

You'll notice that a few of the phrases include the word 'sorry'. I touched on this back in Part 5 on assertiveness (p. 134), and the same idea applies here: you don't have to say sorry, because you're not doing anything wrong by setting a boundary around people-pleasing. That said, people-pleasing often shows up in relationships that matter, and sometimes you really do feel sorry that you can't help. If that's the case, it's okay to express that with the word 'sorry'. Just keep in mind that this kind of 'sorry' isn't about guilt or wrongdoing, it's simply a way of showing that you care.

> 'Can I let you know about that later?'
> 'Sorry, but I'm going to have to pass on that.'
> 'I wish I could help, but I can't this time.'

'I'm feeling really burnt out at the moment – sorry, I have to say no.'

'I can't – I'm taking some much-needed time to rest.'

3. Free yourself from guilt

Guilt is one of the biggest reasons people struggle to stop people-pleasing. To avoid it, people-pleasers often say yes, which might bring temporary relief, but that relief comes at a cost. The good news is you can free yourself from this kind of guilt, and in this section, I'll show you how. Let's start by defining guilt because it isn't always what it seems. In the context of people-pleasing, there are two types of guilt: **healthy guilt** and **unhealthy guilt**, sometimes known as unwarranted guilt.

Before we get into the two types of guilt, it's important to recognize that guilt rarely acts alone. It's often just the tip of the iceberg, beneath which lie deeper feelings: resentment at being placed in a position of obligation, sadness from only feeling valued when you meet others' needs, anxiety about the fallout of saying no, or shame from believing you're uncaring or selfish. In this section, we'll focus on managing guilt since it's the emotion most closely tied to people-pleasing. But don't overlook the possibility of these other feelings being present as well. Always ask yourself, 'Besides guilt, what else am I feeling right now?' Recognizing those other emotions can not only make the guilt less intense, but it can also help you make sense of your experience and process what's going on. It allows you to meet those feelings head-on and give yourself whatever you need to move through them. You might need to sit with what you're feeling, be curious about the feeling, name it, and notice where it shows up in your body.

Write it down. You can ask yourself, if a friend felt this way, what would you say to them or do for them? That's your clue for what to offer yourself. You can also picture having a best friend by your side, who responds to you with the kind of care you'd really want; what would you want them to say or do for you? Whatever that is, do it for yourself. You can also use the 'Feel Your Feelings' exercise (p. 69) to help process your emotions.

Healthy guilt

Healthy guilt shows up when you know you've done something wrong, hurt someone, or made a mistake, whether it was intentional or unintentional. Healthy guilt motivates you to take responsibility for your actions and grow from them. It encourages you to apologize, make amends, explain yourself, and learn from the experience because you don't want it to happen again. All this boosts your integrity and confidence. It also shows others that you care about them, which goes a long way in building trust, respect, happiness and resilience in your relationships.

Unhealthy guilt

Unhealthy or unwarranted guilt is more complicated, and it's the type of guilt most people struggle with. It shows up when you haven't actually done anything wrong but, for some reason, you feel responsible, as if you have. Unhealthy guilt is often out of proportion to the situation. It's the kind of guilt that can weigh heavily on you when you set boundaries, say no, or prioritize yourself, all things that aren't wrong at all. This kind of guilt is unhealthy because it's not based on genuine wrongdoing but on an internal and distorted perception of having failed at something. Sometimes people carry unhealthy guilt from their early life influences. If you grew up in a home where your needs were often brushed aside while you were expected to take care of everyone else, it makes sense that you learned to put yourself last. Life experiences like these can make you believe that other people's needs matter more than yours, and it's your job to look after them. So when you don't, guilt kicks in, even though taking care of yourself isn't wrong, it's absolutely necessary.

Breaking the cycle of unhealthy guilt

When unhealthy guilt takes hold, it can create a cycle that feeds itself. The more you try to please others to avoid feeling guilty, the stronger that pattern becomes, and the more guilt shows up each time you put yourself first or even think about doing so. Each time you give in to guilt and put other people's needs before your own, you strengthen the belief that you have to meet their needs, that they matter more than you and that your worth depends on what you do for them. So you feel compelled to keep doing the same thing, even if you don't feel like you actually want to.

The way out of this is learning to recognize when you're experiencing unhealthy guilt, to name it, see it for what it is, and stop letting it dictate your choices. To figure out which type of guilt you're feeling and how best to handle it, start by asking yourself these questions:

> 'Have I done anything wrong here? If so, what are the facts and actual evidence of what I've done?'
>
> 'If I haven't done anything wrong and no facts support that, could this be unhealthy guilt?'

If it's healthy guilt, do what you need to do to make things right. If it's unhealthy guilt, recognize it for what it is and reframe it by saying: 'This is unhealthy guilt; I haven't done anything wrong. It's not wrong to . . .'

Then take some time to think things through before you decide how to act. Start by looking at what might be underneath the guilt. You can ask yourself: What triggered this feeling? What old patterns or experiences does this remind me of? When else have I felt this way?

Your answers are clues pointing to where this guilt might be coming from. Because often, it's not about the current situation at all. It's old stuff being reactivated. Building that kind of awareness helps you see that you haven't actually done anything wrong, it just feels like you have.

Once you can see what's really going on, it's like having a map in your hands; you know where you are, and how you got there. But knowing this doesn't automatically transport you to where you want to be. You still need to take the next steps to complete that journey of moving away from unhealthy guilt. And here's how you can do that:

Step one

Acknowledge your guilt, even if it's irrational and makes no logical sense. You can do this by saying to yourself, 'I feel guilty, even though I've done nothing wrong, this is unhealthy guilt.'

Step two

Take a moment to think about where your guilt is coming from. Naming the source can help you see where it might come from – it's a reaction to something specific, not a reflection of who you are as a person.

Step three

Now look at what beliefs fuel your guilt by paying attention to the thoughts that appear when you're feeling guilty. Maybe it's, 'I should always put others first.' Then, get curious about those beliefs by asking yourself: 'Is that really how it should be? Does this belief help me? Do I have to keep doing this? What's the best and worst that could happen if I continue living by this belief? What would be a more balanced way of thinking and being?'

Step four

Decide what action you want to take. Ask yourself if unhealthy guilt wasn't calling the shots, what would I actually want to do? 'What choice would feel right for me? What's the best thing for me?' Then do exactly that.

Guilt might still show up when you set a boundary, or say no, especially early on, when you're just starting to untangle yourself from people-pleasing. It's completely normal. When it does, just return to this chapter to remind yourself how to work through it. And remember that if you keep giving in to unhealthy guilt, you won't get the chance to build your ability to handle the discomfort that comes with saying no. And that's such an important part of the process. The more you stick with it, even when it feels hard, the more resilience you can build, which will move you closer to the kind of growth you really want.

4. Deal with self-critical thoughts

As you pull back from people-pleasing, you might notice your inner critic ramping up, trying to steer you back towards old patterns. It's completely normal for a wave of negative, self-critical thoughts to show up when you start making these changes. When that inner critic speaks up don't just accept what it says, get curious and question what it's telling you. You need to check whether it's accurate. If it is, then fine, you can hold onto what it's telling you. But if it's not, let it go, replace it or update it to make it more reflective of truth and reality. A good way to check if a thought is accurate is to look at the evidence for and against it. If the evidence is weak or doesn't add up, that's a red flag. It's a sign that your thought isn't accurate, and you can reframe it.

Reframing is about shifting your perspective, it isn't about replacing a negative thought with an overly positive one, it's about telling yourself the truth. It's about finding a more balanced and grounded way of looking at things. For example, if you think, 'I'm selfish', ask yourself if there's solid evidence that selfishness defines who you are most of the time. If there is, note it down. Then write down the evidence that shows you're not selfish. If the evidence against the thought is strong, that's a good indication it's a thought you need to look at differently – by reframing it. Doing this can help stop your mind telling itself the same old inaccurate story over and over. When you keep doing this you'll notice your inner dialogue starting to shift towards a more balanced, healthier way of seeing things.

Here's an example of how you might reframe a thought about being selfish: 'I'm not selfish; I'm allowed to think about my needs. Prioritizing myself doesn't make me a bad person. In fact, it makes me better able to show up for others when I do.'

And, here are a few more examples of reframing:

> **Original thought:** They'll hate me if I don't help.
> **Reframed thought:** If someone's love depends on me always saying yes, that's a red flag. A healthy relationship is about respect, not just agreeing all the time.
>
> **Original thought:** They won't need me any more if I stop helping so much.
> **Reframed thought:** Healthy relationships are about mutual respect, not just about needing each other all the time. If they only want me because I'm always helping, that's not really healthy.
>
> **Original thought:** If I don't help, everything will fall apart.
> **Reframed thought:** It's not just my job to help. There are other people who can help too, or they can figure out another solution. I'm not responsible for everything.

Chapter 5: What Happens When You Stop People-Pleasing

When you stop people-pleasing, you'll get a mix of reactions, some positive, some negative, some neutral. Some people might feel annoyed, upset or even angry because they no longer get to benefit from your people-pleasing. Don't take their negative reactions as proof that you're doing something wrong or that you're a bad person. If someone gets upset because you're no longer overextending yourself to please them, it's important to know that their reaction might be coming from all sorts of places. From what I've seen in my clinical work it's often because they're struggling with their own psychological difficulties. And you might already have a sense of that, based on what you know about them and how they relate to others. And if you do, it becomes easier to accept that their reaction isn't really about you at all. Sometimes, their reactions can be rooted in confusion, if your shift in behaviour was sudden or unexplained, they might feel like they've done something wrong. Especially if you'd never shared how much of a toll your overextending was taking on you; you may have hidden it well, and they may have had no idea. So try to leave some room for nuance when you're making sense of why they're upset. It's not always about you doing something wrong, and neither is it always about them being a bad person.

If someone's negative reaction doesn't fade over time, or they stop talking to you altogether, it might mean the relationship was never as solid as it seemed, and perhaps it was conditional all along. If so, it wouldn't have lasted anyway. Let them react however they need do, feel whatever they feel and if they stop talking to you, let that be okay too. Their feelings are theirs to deal with, and you can't control that, nor can you control whether they explain themselves or not. That's their choice. If, in their own time, they can work through what they're feeling and come back, ready to respect your boundaries and rebuild a healthier relationship, that's wonderful. But if they don't, it's okay to let the relationship go, sometimes that's the healthiest choice. And it's also okay to move on and focus on the things that matter to you.

Not everyone will react negatively to you stopping people-pleasing – some people will actually support it. Yes, they might be a bit surprised at first, especially if people-pleasing is something you've always done, but they'll understand. They'll support your decision and respect your boundaries. They won't guilt-trip you or get annoyed with you. They also won't stop talking to you, or get angry or upset about your choices. You might even notice that they ask less of you, not because they care less, but because they value you. They understand the shift you're making. Some might even reflect on times when they leaned on you too much and feel the urge to apologize. They might even offer their help and support in return. Healthy people know that meaningful relationships aren't built on one person constantly giving and the other constantly taking. They're built on mutual respect and understanding. So they'll still be there because they care about you, not just what you do for them. And these are exactly the kinds of relationships worth nurturing.

Things to hold onto . . .

People-pleasing is when you put other people's needs or opinions ahead of your own. It's often driven by a fear of disappointing them, being disliked or rejected, or feeling like you're not enough unless you're constantly doing things for others.

Personality traits, early life experiences, trauma, learned behaviours, anxiety or a fear of being fully yourself can all play a part in how people-pleasing takes hold.

People-pleasing often becomes a cycle. You believe you're not enough, so you give more, do more, please more – trying to earn a sense of worth. But because your worth is tied to what you do for others, you never quite feel enough unless you keep doing!

You can move away from people-pleasing by making choices based on your values instead of fear. You can learn to step back from unhealthy guilt and stop over-giving, and when you do, the people who are healthy will still be there for you because they care about you and not just what you can do for them.

Part Seven

How to Deal with Conflict

Knowing how to handle conflict is an essential life skill; it helps you stay calm and clear when things get tricky. As much as we try to keep the peace, conflict still manages to find its way into our lives. Whether it's with friends, partners, colleagues or family, no one gets through life without disagreements. Some of them can be silent tensions, while others can erupt into full-blown, heated arguments. And sometimes differences can spiral so far that they leave lasting hurt and resentment.

Sometimes conflict can be fairly straightforward, uncomfortable, yes, but manageable. However there are also moments of confrontation that feel so unsettling, they make you want to shrink back. And that's especially true when you haven't quite figured out how to deal with them. When you don't know how to deal with conflict, just the thought of it can bring a wave of anxiety. And when you sense it's about to happen, that fear can kick in fast. Each time it happens, it hits the same raw place, the part of you that never really got over what happened last time, making even small conflicts feel overwhelming. Because of this, your emotional response to conflict can be amplified by unresolved past feelings and anxieties. The fear of being hurt again can also cloud your judgement, making it harder to respond the way you'd really like to. You might also fear the reaction of the person you are in conflict with, how you'll feel, what they'll say, and how that will make you feel. Will you be able to say what you want to? How can you make it stop? And how much will it affect you? To cope with these fears, you might become avoidant of conflict; maybe you stay silent, walk away, change the subject, distract yourself or even blame yourself, or them. But every time you avoid conflict, your fear of it grows, and your confidence in dealing with it shrinks.

This is how conflict becomes something you dread. The way to break free from this fear is to step into it, little by little. In this part, I'll give you the tools you need to do just that, so you can learn that conflict isn't as scary as it seems.

Chapter 1:
What Is Conflict?

Conflict happens when people strongly disagree, or when values, expectations or needs don't line up. In those moments, things can quickly become tense and emotionally charged. Everyone involved feels misunderstood or hurt, as if something important to them has been dismissed or challenged. You each stand your ground, convinced your perspective is right and theirs is wrong. Things get heated, stressful and frustrating – and afterwards, you're left feeling drained, wounded, overwhelmed and probably so much more besides. Some of the most common triggers for conflict are:

> Communication problems
> Disagreements about how time is spent
> Disagreements about decisions or opinions
> Clashing needs or expectations
> Broken promises or missed commitments
> Money and finances
> Uneven division of responsibilities
> Differing values or beliefs
> Healthy vs unhealthy habits
> Untidiness or cleanliness

No matter what kind of conflict it is, there's something powerful about finding a way through. This part of the book is about that kind of conflict – the kind that happens when both people respect each other's fundamental rights: the right to be treated with respect, to think and feel differently, to set boundaries, to be heard and to disagree. It's about the right to seek solutions, to take a step back when you need to, to be free from pressure, and most importantly, to feel safe. That's what healthy conflict is: a disagreement with empathy acting as the bridge that keeps both sides connected. Even if they don't see eye to eye, both people want to understand each other's perspective. And they have reasonable expectations of each other. Even when they don't agree, they're willing to step into each other's shoes and look for solutions that work.

This part of the book isn't about people who refuse to work through conflict, those that treat it like a one-way street – it's their way or the highway. They have unrealistic expectations and are completely unwilling to see any perspective but their own. Trying to reason with them is like building a sandcastle against a rising tide, it's futile and destructive. When empathy is missing conflict becomes unhealthy and toxic. We'll look at these harmful patterns in Part 9, where you'll learn how to protect yourself from them.

Chapter 2: Why Conflict Feels So Overwhelming

If conflict leaves you anxious, on edge or ready to shut down, you're not alone. It feels difficult for lots of reasons, and it's not because you're weak or flawed. In this chapter, we'll look at why conflict can feel so threatening. As you read through, notice which reasons resonate most with you.

Overwhelming emotions

Conflict can stir up such a storm of emotions. Like many people, you might struggle with feeling that way. It sends you into a panic, where every word, every shift in tone, every verbal challenge feels like you're being pushed towards a path you don't want to go down. You might be someone who's learned to bottle up emotions because, at some point, showing them wasn't safe. So you suppress your upset, anger, frustration or sadness. And when conflict shows up – with all its emotional intensity – you're terrified of having to face those feelings. You get the instant urge to run, to avoid it at all costs or to make it end as quickly as possible. If this sounds like you, improving your emotional regulation skills can really help. You can do that by using the 'Feel Your Feelings' skill on p. 69. That along with the tools in this chapter, can reduce the fear you have around these intense emotions.

Insecurity and anxiety

Insecurity and anxiety can also make conflict feel overwhelming. They can cloud your perspective, making it hard to have the conversations you know you need to have or wish you could have. If only you didn't feel so afraid of other people's reactions, of being hurt, criticized, disappointing someone or being misunderstood. There's aslo the anxiety of not knowing where the conflict will lead, how badly things could go and how the situation could spiral. The fear of how things could escalate can make it seem easier to avoid a difficult conversation altogether. On top of that, speaking up might feel like you're stirring up more trouble. If you're already insecure or afraid of being judged, the risk of speaking up can feel too high.

Echoes of the past

The way you were raised and your past experiences also shape how you view conflict, including the way you think, feel and react when things with others get tough. If you grew up in a home that was a safe space for disagreements where people calmly talked things through, you probably see conflict as something solvable, not something to fear. But if your past experiences of conflict were chaotic, with yelling, blaming, tension and no productive outcomes, you might feel frightened and intimidated by it. If solutions were rarely found, you might have learned that conflict is pointless. You might have had past experiences where trying to play an active role in solving an issue resulted in you feeling like you were under attack. Maybe you've had past experiences where you walked away thinking you must have said or done something wrong, or maybe someone else did, and they just wouldn't accept it. Over time, you may have come to believe that conflict is simply unpleasant, unsafe and best avoided.

Communication skills

How you communicate with others also plays a big part in whether a conflict gets resolved or spirals out of control. If you're able to communicate well and can take a step back, to process your feelings, gather your thoughts and then express what you need in a way that makes sense to you and to the other person, things can work out well. But when you struggle with these communication skills, the heat of the moment can cloud everything, leaving you unsure of what you even want, let alone putting all that into words.

Conflict Traps

There are four common traps we can fall into when conflict shows up, and getting stuck in them adds to the overwhelm. You might be an *avoider*, quietly sidestepping things; an *accommodator*, trying to smooth things over at your own expense; an *aggressor*, charging headfirst into battle; or a *passive-aggressor*, throwing in subtle jabs for satisfaction. Often, these are just survival mechanisms, ways of coping because, in the heat of the moment, you don't know what else to do. As an *avoider*, you're the type of person who prefers to keep the peace, even if it means pretending nothing's wrong when the truth is you're actually upset. But you'd rather avoid an uncomfortable conversation, telling yourself, 'It's not worth it, just let it slide.' As an *accommodator*, you're someone who puts everyone else's needs first and sets your own aside. In conflict, you might not express your own views at all, you just go along with what's being suggested, while you're quietly suppressing your thoughts and feelings. You say one thing on the outside, while on the inside you're quietly resenting your decision but feel stuck with it. Or you could be the *aggressor*, the person who confronts everything head-on with full force. You want to 'win', and you feel like if you just push your point hard enough, the other person will see your side or give in. You have the false illusion that you're standing your ground and are great at fighting your corner, but while you're doing that you're probably harming your relationships. Lastly, there's the *passive-aggressor*: you don't say what you really mean, but you drop subtle sarcastic or indirect hints, hoping they'll get it. And if they don't? Well at least it might make them feel something negative, so the mission is partially accomplished. But this still breeds resentment, and you're left feeling frustrated at not having expressed yourself properly. None of these responses actually solves conflict; they're all fear-based reactions, that in the moment feel like they protect you from the discomfort of dealing with conflict. But in the long run they prevent you from truly understanding yourself and others. Instead of moving forward and being a collaborator, you're stuck, feeling unheard, frustrated and disconnected from others.

Chapter 3: Handling Conflict with Confidence

In this section, I'll take you through eight practical skills to help you handle conflict with more confidence. You'll learn how to stay emotionally grounded, communicate clearly, understand what you want, be more flexible in your thinking, stand by your values, and know when to step back.

1. Own your feelings

Strong emotions are a natural part of conflict – it's just how it is. It makes sense that people don't feel joyful in these moments, and that emotions can run high. There are so many things that can trigger strong feelings. It might be a fight-flight response, that automatic reaction when you sense a threat. It could be the vulnerability of being exposed or open to the possibility of hurt. Or it could be something the other person does – like the way they speak or behave. Regardless of where these feelings come from, what makes the difference is taking responsibility for them. When you acknowledge and own what you're feeling, you gain more control over yourself. It's like taking the reins of the situation instead of being pulled along. And from there, you can choose a more grounded response, rather than letting strong emotions dictate how you act. So here's what you can do.

Before conflict

Since you've been through conflict before, you probably already know the emotions that tend to come up in those moments. Think about what you typically feel. Is it fear, anger, disappointment or maybe sadness? And where do those emotions show up in your body? Do they feel like a heavy weight on your chest, a tightness in your throat, a knot in your stomach or maybe pressure in your head? Developing an awareness of your typical emotional responses and where you feel them in your body gives you valuable insight. It can help you stay calmer the next time conflict shows up. When you know what to expect – how you'll feel and where – it won't catch you off guard, it won't have that same shock factor. You'll be prepared for it. And when you're prepared, you're more accepting, and that can take away some of the surprise and fear. This can reduce the intensity of those emotions, making the situation feel less unknown and less scary.

During conflict

When conflict arises, expect the very feelings you've recognized to come up. When they do, just notice them – don't try to resist, fight or push them away. Don't react impulsively. Simply sit with them. These feelings are yours, tied to the situation, so just let them be. Slow down and give yourself space to feel them. Don't react with urgency. Let there be pauses as the other person speaks. These moments of stillness give you the time to settle and help prevent your emotions from taking over. It's like slowly putting the brakes on a fast-moving car.

This calm pace also helps you avoid saying something you might regret and increases your ability to tolerate the discomfort of the conflict. It gives both your mind and body time to settle after any initial reaction.

After conflict

After conflict, take a moment to check in with yourself. Are any feelings still hanging around? If so, what are they? Are those feelings making you think negatively about yourself? It's not unusual to leave a conflict with negative thoughts like, 'I'm so weak.' If that happens, see if you can meet the thought with curiosity instead of believing it outright. Ask yourself: 'Is this really true? Am I actually weak most of the time?' If the answer is no, and it just feels like your emotions are exaggerating your negative thoughts, acknowledge that too. You can say to yourself: 'I might have thought that in the moment, but that's not who I am most of the time.' And if you still need to shake off more tension, do something that helps you shift your mindset: go for a walk, listen to music or move your body to release the built-up energy and adrenaline that the conflict might have left you with.

2. Draw your lines

Spending time reflecting on past conflicts is a powerful way to prepare for future ones. It can help you see where you want to set your boundaries so conflict unfolds in a way that feels okay for you. I've laid out some questions below that you can ask yourself to help pinpoint where you might want those limits to be. Whether you've been hurt, overwhelmed, ignored or pushed too far, you can set limits to shape the way future disagreements go. You might be thinking: 'But

I can't control the conflict and what the other person does.' And yes, that might be true, you can't control them, but you are in control of yourself. You can absolutely control how you respond and what you allow. That's where your power lies. Use these questions to get clear on your limits so you know how to shape your choices going forward:

- What words or actions stuck with you most in past conflicts?
- Were you talked over, dismissed or not given enough space to share your thoughts?
- What really got under your skin?
- Did their tone, body language or volume of speech leave you feeling disrespected?
- What are the things you no longer want to tolerate in conflict?
- How do you want to be treated or spoken to when things get heated?
- Did you feel drained afterwards? Maybe you need to think about setting a time limit on these conversations?
- Did you feel heard? How often did you find yourself repeating the same point? Would it help to set a boundary around that?
- Is there anything you said or did that you wish you'd handled differently? What would you do if the same situation came up again?
- Were there things you held back from saying? How can you make sure you speak up next time?

3. Use your values

Your values are your compass, helping you navigate conflict with intention. They give you a clearer sense of who you are, and research has found that when you have that clarity, you're more likely to handle conflict in a positive, constructive way, as well as worrying less about it.[22]

When conflict shows up, let your values guide you. They can help you decide what to say and how to act. As an example, let's say respect is one of your values. Aligning yourself with that during conflict can mean approaching the situation with respect for yourself and for the other person. But it also means respecting yourself by stepping back if the conflict feels disrespectful to you. You can say something like, 'I'm being respectful to you, please be respectful back.' The value of safety is closely linked to the value of respect, so if things become overwhelming and you feel unsafe in any way, it means walking away from that situation. You can say something like, 'I need to take a break from this, I'm feeling uncomfortable.' If honesty is one of your values, it might mean being open in what you say during conflict instead of tiptoeing around the issues. If you're someone who values compassion, it might mean approaching conflict with kindness and understanding – for yourself and the other person. If you live by the value of growth, you might see conflict as a chance to grow, build your confidence and resilience, and improve your relationships. Accountability is another key value when it comes to conflict. It's about recognizing that you might have played a part, and if you did, it's about owning your part in whatever's happened, instead of just placing all the blame on someone else. And if you value being open-minded, you might try to really listen to the other person's side of things, even if you disagree with their perspective. Values shape how you are in conflict in different ways, and they can really help you work your way through it. Aside from the ones I've mentioned, review your own list of values and think about how you can let them guide your words and actions the next time conflict shows up.

4. Understand what you want or need

Understanding and expressing your needs in conflict is part of being true to yourself. Research shows that people who can do this tend to cope better with stress and conflict.[23] That kind of authenticity seems to have a protective effect, softening the emotional toll that conflict can take. So be sure to take a moment to connect with yourself and tune in to what you truly want or need in these moments. Conflict often comes from different needs pulling in different directions, so knowing yours can help you find a way through that feels right for you. You might have an instinctive feeling about what you want or need to happen. Or you might feel pulled towards a certain outcome. But if you're still drawing a blank during conflict, try asking yourself: 'What do I really want here?' If you know, then go for it! But if you're unsure, ask yourself: 'Do I need some time to think this through?' If you do, that's totally fine too. You can say, 'I need some time to think about this; it's a bit too much right now. I'll come back to you.' Then, take a step back, reflect on the situation and get clear on where you stand. When you return, you'll have a much clearer sense of what you want.

Stepping back is more effective than reacting on impulse, just to escape the uncomfortable feeling of being in conflict. If you give in because you want the tension to end, you might lose sight of your needs. You could end up agreeing to something you'll kick yourself for later. But when you know what you want, you can steer the conversation towards your needs, and hopefully theirs too, or meet them halfway. This also means other people can't push you around or take advantage of you being unsure. Here are some more questions to help you think about what you might want:

- What do I really want to happen?
- Does what I want line up with my values and what I need?
- How can I meet them halfway?
- What matters to me in the short term and long term?
- Will I be proud of the choice I'm making?
- How much energy and time do I want to give this?
- Do I want to let this go?

5. The power of listening

One of the smartest and most transformative ways to deal with conflict is to listen. And this isn't about listening just so you can fire back, it's about listening in a way that makes the other person feel genuinely heard. Conflict isn't just about getting what we want, it's also about people feeling understood. Conflict tends to escalate when people don't feel listened to, it's like being told, 'You're not important, you don't matter, I don't care. I'm just focused on my way.' Being dismissed like this is hugely painful for most of us. When we don't feel listened to, it can also make us defensive, and that defensiveness can push us to react in harsh ways, even if we don't want to.

When someone listens properly, it's like they're saying, 'I understand you. I get what you're saying. I respect you, and I really want to understand your point of view.' That can instantly calm things down because the other person feels understood, respected and heard. And when that happens they're much more open to hearing your side of things, too.

So, how do you listen properly? It's not just about hearing the words the other person is saying, it's also about understanding what they're feeling. Ask them, 'How do you feel about that?' Ask them what they think would help. Ask them, 'What do you want to happen?' It doesn't mean you're giving in; it means you're listening with real empathy and using strong conflict resolution skills. By doing this, you're making the conflict feel less like a fight.

Sometimes, listening also means being open to feedback. The other person might be trying to give you well-intentioned, valuable feedback, but if it lands as criticism, it can turn into conflict. Has that ever happened to you? Or maybe the other way around, when you've tried to give feedback? When you're really listening, it's easier to tell whether they're offering something helpful or just swinging at you. Good feedback has a warmth to it; it's not about making you feel small or attacking who you are as a person. It's more like saying, 'Here's another way to do things.'

It might still be tough to hear, especially if it makes you feel like you're not good enough. But when that happens, ask yourself: 'Are they really saying I'm not good enough overall?' Also: 'Could what they're saying help me be better at something?' It probably wasn't easy for them to bring it up, and it can help to recognize that they care enough to say it. If their intention is to support you, the person who benefits most is actually you. Being open to feedback, even when it's uncomfortable or triggers insecurities, is exactly how we grow. So, really listen and see if there's something useful in there for you. If there is, try to accept it. If it's hard to hear in the moment, you can always say, 'Thanks for the feedback. I'm going to think about that.'

6. Your body language and voice

Your tone of voice, body language and how you say things can either calm a conflict or blow things up. When emotions are running high, your tone of voice can change and so can your volume. The other person can mirror this, or vice versa, and soon, you're no longer solving the problem, you're just reacting to each other's stress. A calm, measured tone can help ease the tension in conflict faster than you might think, making the roughest of waters feel more like gentle ripples. This can help the disagreement become more of a conversation, moving away from an emotionally charged exchange to a productive one. On the other hand, a harsh or aggressive tone is like fanning the flames of a fire. People sometimes come to conflict ready to fight, so if your tone and body language show them you're calm and the situation is safe, they can drop their fight, and again, things can become more constructive.

If, during the conflict, you notice your tone shifting, take a moment to pause. Let the other person keep talking, and use that time to take some slow, deep breaths. You can also focus on something neutral in the room to shift your focus away from the tension so it breaks the cycle of escalating emotions. You can also practise lowering your voice, slowing your speech, or use pauses, by taking a breath after each sentence, to really slow things down.

If you have defensive body language, if you're crossing your arms, staring someone down, making angry or aggressive faces, or pacing around, you're telling them, 'I'm ready to fight.' And guess what? They're probably going to get into fight mode back with you. But if you present with relaxed open body language without crossing your arms, making softer eye contact, a softer face, it shows your willingness and openness to meet them where they're at. When you think about your delivery, body language and facial expressions, imagine looking at yourself in a mirror. What do you want to see in a moment of conflict? Try to show that to the other person. This isn't about giving in, and it definitely doesn't mean you're letting someone walk all over you. It's about you choosing how you want to show up, and how you want to feel during conflict. It's you taking control, holding your ground, and doing it with grace. And this can change the whole tone, making conflict feel more like a conversation.

The words you choose also matter. If you want to keep things calm and get to a solution, using 'I' statements is more effective. They focus on your feelings rather than making the other person feel blamed or attacked. When someone says, 'You always do this!' or 'I can't believe you did that!' what's your first instinct? Probably to get defensive, right? But if they say, 'I felt upset when XYZ happened because . . .' it hits differently. It doesn't feel like an attack, more like an honest expression of a feeling. Feelings aren't debatable, nobody can argue with your feelings. If you say you feel upset, then that's your inner experience, it can't be denied or argued with. Feelings just are! Taking this approach based on your feelings often leads to a more constructive and empathetic conversation, which can make it easier and quicker to get to a solution.

7. Finding your higher ground

Conflict can feel like a battlefield. You feel under attack, they fire shots through harsh words, personal digs or accusations. And your first instinct might be to fire back. But that only makes it worse, it adds more fuel to the fire. You get the exact opposite of what you really want – which is for the stress to be over.

But why do some people do this, while others don't? It's easy to assume the other person is out to get you, but there's often more to it than that. Struggling with impulse control is one possibility, reacting before thinking about the consequences of what you're saying or doing. You can also be more vulnerable to lashing out in these ways if you struggle with handling intense emotions. Some people lash out because they think their ego or sense of worth is under attack; some people may appreciate you when you don't feel like a threat to their ego or insecurities, but can lash out in retaliation or punishment when you challenge them. Others do it because they want to dominate the argument, they see conflict as something they have to win, be in control of, or they want to steer things to go in their favour. They think being harsh and offensive will get them there, but it won't. It just digs the divide deeper. It becomes a downward spiral of negativity, making conflict more intense and harder to resolve, and, in the end, both sides walk away feeling drained and defeated.

When you're continually dealing with conflict by hitting back in these ways, you're also reinforcing the habit of reacting like that, making it feel normal. It can train your mind to believe that this is how you should be in conflict, and at the first trigger, the boxing gloves come on again. You might get a short burst of satisfaction from 'putting them in their place', or they might from putting you in yours, but if the problem is still unresolved, have you really succeeded?

If things do escalate, there are ways you can bring back calm. Your first step is noticing it's happened. Accept that your reaction might have added fuel to the fire, which can happen to all of us. Own your part in it by saying something honest, like, 'I shouldn't have said that. I don't want this to escalate. I'm sorry. Let's get back to trying to figure this out. What do you think would help most?' You can also shift your body language and tone of voice, soften both, go back to using 'I' statements, and step away from blame. Acknowledge how they're feeling, even if you don't agree with their view. You can say something like, 'I can see that you're really upset.' If none of that seems to land and emotions are still running high, suggest a break. You can say something like, 'This is feeling too intense. Let's take a breather and come back when we're both calmer, so we can really understand each other.' All of this can help bring things back from the brink. It shows you're not trying to win a fight, you're trying to get back to a place where you can really talk things through.

Real strength isn't in how loudly you argue or how good you are at making people back down, but in how well you stay grounded, stand firm, keep your dignity, remain respectful and as calm as you can. This isn't weakness, it's self-control. It's you choosing your higher ground, to rise above the chaos rather than getting dragged into it. Even if the other person throws jabs, you don't have to throw them back. You can choose not to engage in that type of negativity. When you do so, you show them that you value solving the conflict more than fighting or being right, which creates space for a healthier solution and often helps them back down.

8. Recognize everyone's truth

From my decades of experience as a psychologist, one thing I can say with confidence is this: there's no single truth in how people see things – there's your truth, and there's everyone else's. We often think there's just one truth, and we want to get others to see it. But there's never just one truth. The more people there are, the more truths there are about the *thing* that's been experienced. So recognize everyone's truth, and their right to have it. It's like being in one of those rooms full of mirrors; each person reflects a different angle of the exact moment. Absolute facts are facts, but how we feel about them and how they land with us is entirely personal. Each of us has a different experience of things, with different thoughts, feelings and perspectives about it. And everyone involved is entitled to their truth, thoughts and feelings. Accepting that everyone has their truth doesn't just make conflict easier, it makes life easier. You don't need to convince the other people of your truth, you need to know that they have their version, just like you have yours. People can argue their version until the cows come home, but it won't change how someone else felt and experienced that situation – and nor should it!

When you accept this, you stop getting caught in the 'I'm right, they're wrong' tug-of-war over who is right. The reason these kinds of arguments never get resolved is simple: there's never just one truth. Their experience being different from yours doesn't diminish yours, nor does it mean yours is wrong. It's like saying, 'Okay, I get that's how you saw it, I saw it like this . . .' It's appreciating their reflection in those mirrors and knowing theirs doesn't cancel out yours. The focus can then be on finding common ground where everyone feels heard and respected. Be okay with letting them hold whatever version or story they have, just as you hold yours.

Things to hold onto . . .

Conflict, disagreement and confrontation can feel so overwhelming that it makes you want to shrink away. Especially when you haven't figured out how to handle it effectively.

When conflict shows up you might become an avoider, quietly trying to sidestep the issues. You might accommodate by smoothing things over to keep the peace. You might meet it with aggression, ready to fight. Or you might be passive-aggressive, using subtle jabs that feel satisfying in the moment but don't actually resolve a thing.

Handling conflict with confidence starts with owning your feelings. It means being prepared, knowing how to set limits and staying connected to what matters most to you.

It's also about finding your own higher ground, and remembering that everyone comes with their own truth, and there's rarely just one right way of seeing things.

Part Eight

Letting Go of Unhealthy Comparison

Comparing ourselves to others is something we all do; it's part of being human. Sometimes, without even realizing it, we start measuring ourselves against everyone else. It can look like everyone has it easier, looks better or just seems more confident. You might catch yourself thinking about how they're younger, more attractive, more interesting and it gets you down. Or you might wonder why everything feels so hard for you while it looks like everyone else is gliding through life effortlessly. Scrolling through social media might make you feel like everyone's having more fun than you. Seeing perfect photos or fabulous holidays, you might find yourself questioning why your life isn't like that. You notice how financially comfortable other people seem, while you might be struggling. Even walking past strangers in public, you might catch yourself comparing the way they look, the way they carry themselves, even material things like the car they drive or the clothes they're wearing, and then feeling like you come up short. At work, it's a similar thing. Someone else speaks confidently in meetings, they seem completely at ease, while you're anxious and struggling to find your words.

All these moments show how unhealthy comparison can take hold. In this part of the book, we'll explore the differences between healthy and unhealthy comparison. You'll also learn why unhealthy comparisons hurt so much and, most importantly, how you can start letting go of them so you can finally start to feel better about yourself.

Chapter 1:
What Is Self-Comparison?

Self-comparison is the invisible ruler you use to measure your worth and value against everyone else's. Self-comparison is such a natural human tendency that it's almost like a reflex or a fundamental human program running in all our minds. We compare everything: how attractive we are, how we come across, our style, how we dress, how intelligent we are. We compare our job to their job, their house, how happy they seem, their relationships, how physically fit they are, the things they own, the holidays they go on and how they spend their free time. Some of it's conscious, you know you're doing it, but some of it happens without you even realizing it. Which can be like carrying an invisible backpack loaded with everyone else's 'perfect' things. At first, you barely notice the weight, but over time it starts to drag you down.

I'm sure you've heard it said more times than you can remember: 'Don't compare yourself to others.' It's one of the most useless pieces of advice out there. If only it were that simple, and you could stop doing it. I'm telling you that it's an entirely natural human tendency, that research has confirmed many times over.[24] So, if it's something so ingrained, how should you stop it? The truth is you can't just stop it. And another truth is that self-comparison isn't entirely bad; it can actually be helpful when you do it in a healthy way, and as you read on you'll learn how to do this.

Chapter 2:
Why You Compare Yourself

There are countless reasons why you might fall into the trap of unhealthy self-comparison, and most of it comes down to feeling like you're just not good enough. That belief can take root early in childhood or show up later in life when something happens that shakes your confidence. Your early experiences in childhood are like the first draft of your self-image. It's the foundation of how you see yourself and navigate life with others. It's also when unhealthy comparisons can begin. It can start with parents saying things like, 'Why can't you be more like your brother?' or 'What's wrong with you?' Some parents might say these things with good intentions, but they might have set the bar too high, making you feel like you're chasing a moving target. Words like these can leave a mark even if they weren't intended to hurt you; they can plant the seeds of self-doubt.

Teachers can do a similar thing, intentionally or unintentionally, by highlighting the achievements of others, making you measure yourself against them. Regardless of where it happens, growing up with these kinds of comparisons and criticisms can make you believe your worth depends on how you stack up against others. Once that belief gets deeply embedded, it's like background music playing, always there. Beyond home and school, and even as an adult, you're still chasing that gold star, seeking approval from friends, partners or colleagues driven by those internalized voices from the past.

This sense of not being good enough can easily slip into perfectionism, but you don't have to be a textbook perfectionist to make unhealthy comparisons. If you are a perfectionist, you might be constantly scanning for flaws so you can fix them. People think perfectionism is a good thing, a badge of honour, but behind it, there's often a lot of pain rooted in insecurity. Perfectionism is really a trap because there's never an endpoint. Your mind is constantly consumed with thoughts like, 'How can this be better? How can I improve this? It's just not good enough unless it's perfect.' And even when you think it's perfect, you find a flaw, then you're right back to telling yourself it's not good enough.

There's also the ever-present influence of social media. With people showing off their best life, it's so easy to get sucked into comparing yourself to almost everything you see. You look and wonder, 'Why isn't my life like that? Why don't I look like that? Why don't I eat like that?' Or 'Why don't I have as many followers or likes as they do?' And even though it's often said on social media and elsewhere that social media is fake, and you know that it's a carefully crafted illusion, it still has the power to play with your emotions because it taps into your deep need to feel like you are enough. As a clinician I can tell you that behind the screen, those people you want to be like are struggling with the very same insecurities as you. That said, social media isn't all bad when it comes to comparison. Research shows that being selective about what's consumed and how the comparisons are made can actually be linked to better well-being. So, it's not about avoiding social media, but about how you engage with it and how you choose your comparisons.[25]

Once you're in the habit of unhealthy comparison, it's a

loop. You feel bad, so you compare, and then you feel worse. Sometimes you might even compare, hoping to find proof that you are enough, but it never seems to come. Your brain might even seek comparisons confirming your insecurities because it's wired to seek what's familiar, even if it's uncomfortable or makes you feel bad. Your brain is also designed to conserve energy, and one way it does that is by sticking to patterns and behaviours it already knows, regardless of whether they're helpful. It may seem counter-intuitive, but this is actually a survival mechanism; our brains learn that it's safe to stick with what we know, even if it doesn't feel good. But the amazing thing about our brains is they're also incredibly adaptable. We have neuroplasticity, meaning our brains can change; you can rewire old patterns and habits. Yes, it takes time and effort, but it's totally possible. You can retrain your brain, shifting it away from unhealthy comparison and replacing it with healthier patterns.

Chapter 3:
The Cost of Unhealthy Comparison

Unhealthy self-comparison doesn't just come from insecurity and low self-worth – it feeds them, and this can be the source of many other problems, too. It can leave you vulnerable to other mental health struggles. It can be anxiety, where you're in an almost constant grip of worry about how you measure up, whether you're good enough, or if others are judging you. The more you compare, the more behind you feel, and that pressure can turn into overwhelm, sadness or even depression. When you're always focused on what you don't have or where you think you're falling short, it reinforces the belief that you're not good enough. And the more entrenched that belief gets the more it drains the joy from your achievements, making even your proudest moments feel like nothing special because someone else is doing better. It's a little bit like pouring water into a cup with holes: no matter how much you achieve, comparison makes it feel small and less significant.

I've seen time and again how unhealthy self-comparison can take a serious toll on body image too. People compare their faces and bodies to the 'perfect' pictures they see online, feeling intense pressure to change themselves to match those unrealistic ideals, enhancements or simply the fact that someone is youthful. Youth is temporary for everyone. The fresh, glowing faces you see today will also one day get wrinkles, pores and all the other perfectly normal things that come with time. None of us is immune to this kind of change. But when you get caught in body-based self-comparison, it can push you towards unhealthy habits – restricting food, obsessing over macros, extreme dieting, disordered eating, compulsive exercise or even cosmetic procedures – all in a desperate bid to close the gap between yourself and those 'perfect' bodies.

Unhealthy comparison doesn't just distort how you see yourself, it can easily pull you away from who you really are. When you measure yourself against people whose values you don't even know, you start chasing a version of success that might not even align with what you're about. It's like outsourcing your identity to someone else. You end up making choices based on what will help you keep up with others instead of what will make you happy. When you catch yourself comparing yourself to others, pause and say aloud: *'This is my life, and I get to shape what matters in it.'* Throughout this chapter, you'll find affirmations like this one; use them whenever you need. You can also use them as inspiration to create your own, making them more personal. A meaningful and fulfilling life comes from staying true to your own values, not moulding yourself to be like someone else. When you compare yourself unfavourably to others, their achievements, looks and possessions, you let those comparisons steer your life instead of living authentically, as the real you, the version of you that exists when no one else is watching.

Then there are jealousy and envy, two emotions that nobody likes to admit having, but almost everyone feels. Jealousy kicks in when you fear losing something you have, and envy is when you notice something someone else has and wish it was yours. For some people envy can come with bitterness, but other times it's just a quiet longing. Both jealousy and envy are rooted in insecurity, which is why most people avoid acknowledging them. Admitting to these feelings can feel like admitting you're insecure and not good enough, which is exactly what makes them sting so much. So, it makes sense that you wouldn't want to expose yourself in that way if you're already feeling insecure, right? Jealousy and envy are natural human emotions, they only become a problem if you act on them in a harmful way. If left unchecked, they can turn into anger, whether it's at yourself for not being or doing better, anger at others for having what you want, or even anger at the world for not giving you the same opportunities. That anger can take different forms. Sometimes it turns inward, fuelling self-criticism and feelings of self-hatred that lead to destructive behaviours. Other times, it turns outward, causing resentment that strains your relationships, whether it's through passive-aggression, sarcasm, gossip or conflict.

When you compare yourself and feel like you fall short, you might also worry about how others perceive you. That fear can block you from forming genuine connections. When you're focused on hiding the parts of yourself you think aren't 'good enough', it can lead to feelings of loneliness and isolation. Unhealthy comparison can also destroy your motivation. When you see how great everyone else seems to be doing, it can make you hold back from even trying, because it feels like it'll never be as good. It's like staring up at a mountain and convincing yourself there's no point in climbing it because you'll never reach the top.

The fear of failure, the fear of judgement, the fear of not being as good as others can be paralysing. It holds you back. You procrastinate on things you really want to do because you're so caught up in self-evaluation and comparison that taking a risk feels impossible. The more you compare, the more certain you become that you'll fail. The effort feels too much, not just because of the distance between where you are and where you want to be, but also because of the intensity of the feelings you have when you think of it. So, you don't even want to try. Instead of focusing on small, meaningful goals for yourself, you get stuck thinking, 'Why bother? I'll never be that good anyway.' And that kind of thinking doesn't just slow you down – it can convince you that you're not worthy of success or happiness, that you may as well just go back to accepting that you'll always feel bad about yourself.

Chapter 4: Choosing Healthy Self-Comparison

Healthy self-comparison is about looking at others and feeling inspired. It's about seeing something in someone else that sparks something in you – something that prompts you to improve and grow. Healthy comparison can help you step out of your comfort zone, set goals that actually excite you; you feel motivated and you can't wait to get going. And research shows that the right kinds of comparisons can motivate people to work harder.[26] Connect with this mindset by using this affirmation: *'I compare to be inspired, not to tear myself down.'* Healthy self-comparison also helps you see where you want to be, and what part of your life you need to work on in order to get there. By comparing yourself in a healthy, constructive and fair way, you create a more positive sense of yourself too. In this part, I'll share seven practical skills to help you make sure self-comparison works for you, not against you.

1. Compare yourself using your values

Your values are at the heart of everything when it comes to living a fulfilling life. Your values are your compass, guiding your choices and direction, including how you compare yourself to others and who you compare yourself to. That's why values-driven comparisons can be a powerful way to make sure your self-comparison is healthy, intentional and actually helps you. Values-driven comparisons can guide you to focus on the achievements, qualities, skills or milestones you genuinely appreciate, the things you'd like to grow into yourself. So how do you go about this?

First, get your list of values (see pp. 42–5). Second, the next time you catch yourself making a comparison, pause and ask yourself these two questions:

> 'Does what I'm comparing myself to align with any of my values? If so, which one?'
>
> 'Is this comparison motivating me towards something I actually care about? If so, what, or which value?'

These questions are like a filter; they help you separate the comparisons that serve you from those that don't. If a comparison doesn't align with your values or is unlikely to lead you towards something meaningful, you can let it go. Say to yourself, 'That's not something that fits with what I value, so it doesn't need to take up space in my mind.' And if the comparison has stirred something up in you, whether it's insecurity, frustration or a twinge of envy, acknowledge that too.

One way to tell if a comparison aligns with your values is to pay attention to how it feels. A healthy comparison usually sparks something lighter, a sense of inspiration, motivation, even excitement. There's a warmth to it, and a pull towards something you'd like to grow into. You feel drawn towards what you see, and you feel eager to think about how you can create something similar for yourself.

As an example, let's say you value growth, and you see a friend doing well in their career. You might feel motivated to work on your own career, because what you see in them aligns with your own value of professional growth. You feel positive and excited about what you could also achieve.

But when a comparison clashes with your values, it can leave you with negative emotions, insecurity, resentment, frustration, anxiety and that sinking feeling of not being good enough. For example, you see an influencer showcasing yet another shiny new product or clothing. It makes you think that you should have those things too. It also makes you think your stuff is a bit drab. But emotionally, you feel uncomfortable or annoyed because it contradicts your value of financial stability. And also your value of sustainability, which leads to you feeling frustrated at being influenced to want things that represent excessive consumerism. Instead of getting caught in those emotions, use them as a signal, a clue that tells you, 'This isn't a comparison worth holding onto.' You can also take this a step further by noting the kinds of comparisons that tend to trigger those feelings and make a deliberate choice to limit your exposure to them. For instance, you could do a social media audit, where you review who or what you're following and remove or mute accounts that make you feel worse about yourself.

By weaving your values into the way you make comparisons, you shift comparison from being a source of self-doubt into a tool that moves you towards building a life that feels meaningful and is on your own terms.

2. Create boundaries around self-comparison

You get to choose what enters your inner world. When comparing yourself to others impacts your self-worth, it's your cue to set boundaries. These boundaries can help you stay connected to the person you want to be without letting external comparisons dictate how you feel. Boundaries help you stay aligned with your values, protect your mental space and keep your focus where it matters. Here's another affirmation to help with that, say it out loud: *'I get to choose what influences my thoughts and feelings.'*

Research shows that social comparison can have both positive and negative effects.[27] When a comparison leaves you feeling bad, that's your signal to step away and limit your exposure. Let's say you're scrolling through social media, looking at posts from friends, influencers or someone else. And you come across something that suddenly makes you feel bad about yourself. You can use this as your sign to limit your exposure. This isn't about avoiding reality – it's about being intentional with what you allow in. Protecting your well-being by setting limits on draining comparisons helps you feel emotionally safe, secure and confident, it's like having a personal shield. And when you're not being dragged down by negativity, you have the mental energy to focus on what matters to you for your personal growth. Here's some questions to help you think about the limits you might want to set:

- Think about the times when specific comparisons left you feeling bad. Who were you comparing yourself to?
- What hit hardest about those comparisons?
- Was it a particular person, a specific body type, a material possession? Or something else?

Your answers can give you clarity on what triggers painful comparisons. When you know these, you can set boundaries that give you some distance from them. For example, Aisha kept looking at athletes' six-pack abs because she really wanted abs too. She'd been trying for over a decade and gave it her all. But eventually she realized that getting those visible abs had a lot to do with genetics. Even with consistent effort, it would still be very tough for her to get there. Aisha came to terms with the fact that everyone's muscles and body composition are built differently. Some people store fat elsewhere; others have naturally prominent abdominal tendons that make their abs more visible, and some have naturally shallow, concave bellies. Aisha decided to stop looking at those images because it was a battle she couldn't win, it was just draining her.

Another important boundary to set is choosing not to check up on people from your past, whether it's a friend, an ex, an old colleague, someone from school or someone else – especially when you know it makes you feel bad, like you're falling behind. You might think, 'Let me just see what they're up to so I can figure out how I'm doing in comparison.' Then you google them, see what they're up to, compare that to your own life, and then you feel bad. The urge to make these comparisons usually pops up when you're already feeling low about your own situation. Which is exactly the time to stay away from anything that can make you feel worse. Comparing yourself to them won't move you forward; but it can keep you stuck. One way to set this boundary is to step back from looking them up. Instead of focusing on where they are, focus on how far you've come. Look back at where you were six months ago, a year ago, or longer, and mark your progress. Use the urge to look them up as a trigger to shift your focus and use that time to focus on where you want to go next.

Don't waste your energy on someone who only makes you feel worse. Put them on your mental 'no-go' list – like a blocked number for your peace of mind. If, despite knowing all this, you still get the urge to look up someone, pause for a moment, take a breath, and notice the pull. Then, do something else. Your brain gravitates towards what's familiar, especially when you're feeling vulnerable, so doing something else can break this pattern. You don't have to follow the pull. You get to choose what happens next. Take control of your conscious actions. Checking what someone else is doing is a conscious behaviour because you're engaging in something you're aware of. For example, you have to physically pick up your phone or type on your computer. Recognizing that you control these behaviours gives you the power to create obstacles that protect your peace. The more you interrupt the pattern, the weaker it becomes. You can log out, mute the account, hide it, do what you need to do to keep your attention and energy for things that nourish you.

You can also set boundaries around how often you engage in healthy comparisons. You don't have to compare yourself constantly. You can make comparison something you choose, not something that hijacks your day. You can make it part of a routine, for instance, once a week, where you spend time reflecting on the comparisons that uplift you. By setting limits on comparison, you also give yourself more time and energy to invest in other activities that are equally important in nurturing your growth and well-being.

3. Turn envy into advantage

Addressing the envy that comes with self-comparison is crucial because it can eat away at you. It can keep you stuck in negativity and become the very thing that blocks your growth. When you're fixated on what others have, you can end up spending more time in that headspace than you do actually moving forward. In this section, I'm going to show you how to deal with envy, so you can focus on your own progress instead.

Envy is an unpleasant and painful blend of feelings characterized by inferiority, hostility and resentment, caused by comparison with a person or group of people who possess something you desire.[28] It's when you feel bad because someone else has something you want. There are two types of envy: benign envy, which is when you feel envious and wish you could have what they have, and malicious envy, where you actually wish that person would lose what they have so you can feel better about yourself.[29]

But here's the surprising thing, as unpleasant as it feels, envy can actually be very useful. It's a signpost that helps you recognize what you might want for yourself. A lot of the time, envy has some admiration hidden underneath it, a clue that you've seen something that matters to you, something you want to build into your own life. You're not just upset about what they have, what really stings is realizing that it's something you admire and value but haven't quite gotten yet, or maybe didn't even know mattered to you until someone sparked it in you. And that makes envy powerful. It can show you exactly where to grow. You can reframe it as insight that guides you towards what matters to you, turning it into productive action.

Without action, envy can spiral, leaving you feeling hopeless. Left unchecked, it can breed more insecurity, making it seem like success is out of reach. It's like standing at the starting line but convincing yourself the race is already lost before you've taken a single step. But, instead of beating yourself up, you can use that feeling as a guide to help figure out what really matters to you, and then make a plan to achieve those things. You might not be able to stop envy from showing up, but you do get to decide what you do with it when it does. This is within your control. You can let it weigh you down or you can use it as fuel to move forward, the choice is yours.

Instead of seeing someone else's success as something you'll never achieve, or thinking it somehow takes away from your potential, you can see it as proof of possibility. If they can have and do those things, it's a sign that you can have or do those things too. The next time envy starts creeping in, take a moment to pause and affirm, *'Envy reveals what I value, I can use that to fuel my growth.'*

That affirmation is a starting point, but to really work with envy, it helps to go a little deeper. You can use the questions that follow to turn envy into insight, and shift your focus from unhealthy comparisons to productive self-reflection. When you go through them, please keep in mind that success isn't just about climbing a ladder or accumulating accomplishments. It's also about what feels meaningful to you.

> What is it about this person or situation that really speaks to me?
>
> What are they doing that I'd like to do to?
>
> What is this feeling of envy trying to tell me about what I value or want in my life?
>
> What is the skill they have that I wish I had too?
>
> Am I putting more energy into comparing than creating?
>
> What plan can I make to work towards the things I want?
>
> What's one small step I can take towards building what I want?

The aim isn't to copy someone else's life and try to be just like them. It's about using their achievement as inspiration to create your own version of success that fits with your values. Take what you've learned and turn it into realistic doable goals that actually mean something to you. Don't just think about it, make space for it too. Set aside dedicated time each week to work on these things, even if it's just ten minutes to start with. Starting small can make a big difference.

4. Tame negative self-comparison thoughts

Even when you're focusing on only making healthy self-comparison, negative thoughts can still pop up, it's completely normal and to be expected, especially in the beginning. The kinds of thoughts that usually show can be linked with <u>insecurity</u>, like:

'I'm just not good enough.'

'They're way more successful than I'll ever be.'

'Seems like everyone else has their life sorted, except me.'

<u>Then there are thoughts with pangs of envy:</u>

'It's not fair they have all that.'

'I wish my life was like theirs.'

'Ugh, I'm so envious.'

<u>There are also thoughts filled with self-criticism or anxiety:</u>

'What's wrong with me?'

'I never get anything right.'

'I'll never find happiness.'

<u>And of course, the body image thoughts:</u>

'I wish I looked like that.'

'I feel so wrinkly and ugly.'

'I feel so unfit.'

If you have these kinds of thoughts, don't be alarmed, and don't assume they are fact. You're not alone in experiencing thoughts like these, everyone has them from time to time. As you practise making healthier comparisons, they'll show up less and less. What really matters is how you respond when they do. Here's how you can work with those thoughts.

Step 1: Accept it. First of all, just accept that these thoughts will show up, and tell yourself it's okay if they do. It doesn't mean there's anything wrong with you. They're just mental noise, not messages of truth. Acknowledge them without judgement. You can do that by saying to yourself: 'I'm having the thought that . . .' and describe it. Don't try to push them away or wrestle with them, just let them be. Pay attention to them without letting them dictate your actions. Thoughts like these can trick you into doing things that make them even stronger, but remember, these thoughts are not facts. They're like actors on a stage, they can perform all they like, you don't have to buy into the script. Acting on them only gives them more power, it makes them feel real, which means they'll come back again and again. For example, if your thought is, 'Everyone's more successful than me', don't start searching for proof. That's like watering seeds, you're only helping the thought take root and spread deeper.

Step 2: Shift your focus. Rather than getting fixated on the thought, shift your attention to something else. Dwelling on it signals to your mind that you think it's important, it's like putting a spotlight on a shadow, it grows bigger. The more you focus on it, the more ingrained it can become, meaning it will show up more and more, and when it does, it can make your brain treat it as fact. One way to interrupt this process is to do something that gently shifts your mindset: go for a walk, phone a friend, listen to a favourite song, anything that helps change the frequency your brain is tuned in to. And remind yourself: 'I am in charge of how I respond to my thoughts.'

Step 3: Turn thoughts into action. If you think there's something constructive you can take from the thought, come back to it later, when you feel less consumed by it. For example, if your thought is 'I feel so unfit', it might mean that you want to improve your fitness. If that's the case, make a plan for that. What do you want to do? How often? When do you want to start? And so on. Then put your plan into action. But remember – not every thought deserves a reaction. Some are just like passing clouds. So save your energy for the thoughts that shine a light on something real and possible. Action planning is only for the ones that actually point you towards something you can improve or change.

5. Process your emotions

With every painful thought come painful feelings. When you compare yourself to others, emotions like insecurity, anxiety, sadness, envy, anger can surface. Sometimes these feelings are tied to old insecurities. When a current situation triggers an emotion similar to a past experience, it can also bring back those old feelings. It's part of why these emotions can feel so intense, even disproportionate when you consider the current trigger. You're not just feeling this moment, you can be carrying every moment that felt like this one before. If that's the case, working through what you're feeling now also helps you process some of the old stuff. Managing these feelings each time they show can be a game changer. Here's how you can do that using the 'Six Steps to Emotional Calm':

1. Understand and accept that discomfort will show up. It's a natural part of the process. It might feel intense in the moment, but it's temporary and will always fade. Say out loud: *'I allow emotional discomfort to come and go, knowing that it's part of my healing.'*

2. Tune into your internal state. Ask yourself, 'What am I feeling right now?' Is it envy, insecurity, frustration or something else? There might be more than one feeling, so acknowledge them all without judgement.

3. Locate your emotions, don't just think the emotion, feel where it lands. Where do you feel it in your body? Do your feelings sit like a weight in your chest, a knot in your stomach or a lump in your throat? Or do they show up somewhere else; if so, where?

4. Give your feelings a colour, turn that invisible feeling into something visual. If your emotions had a colour, what would it be? Red, blue, black, grey – choose a colour that best represents what you're feeling.

5. Observe it. Picture the feeling sitting in that part of your body, in the colour you've given it. Observe it, not to judge it, not to fight it, just to see what happens to it. Does it move? Soften? Change? The simple act of noticing it can give you space from it.

6. Identify what the emotion needs. Ask yourself, 'What would soothe this feeling?' If it's restless or heavy, maybe movement could help, such as stretching, walking,

dancing or shaking it out. If you're feeling insecure, what things remind you of your strengths? What words or past moments can you reconnect with to ground yourself in your own worth? Whatever the emotion needs, try to meet that need with care.

6. Choose compassion over criticism

Healthy self-comparison means stepping away from that relentless inner critic and leaning into self-compassion. Research shows that people with higher self-compassion tend to compare themselves less to others and worry less about how they're perceived.[30] We all know that harsh critical voice in our heads, it's loud, persistent, and always ready to tear us down. It's closely tied to unhealthy comparison because it thrives on making you feel inadequate. That critical voice doesn't just fuel comparison, it can drag you back into it. It fixates on your perceived flaws, zooming in on them like a magnifying glass, filling your mind with everything you supposedly lack. That's where self-compassion comes in. Instead of letting comparison be a tool for self-punishment, it supports you to turn it into something fair and helpful, something that actually helps you grow. Think of self-compassion as the voice of your kindest, most understanding ally, or friend. Self-compassion doesn't demand perfection, it reminds you of your humanity, and that you're doing the best you can. The critical voice might push you towards chasing unattainable standards, but the compassionate one knows that everyone has vulnerabilities that make things hard. Instead of tearing you down, it nurtures those soft spots, offering encouragement so you can move forward in a way that actually works for you.

When that self-critical voice starts blaring like a broken

record, self-compassion is there to hit the mute button, or at least turn the volume down. Affirm this by saying: ***'I turn down the volume of my inner critic and turn up the voice that believes in me and encourages me.'*** A really helpful way to lean in to self-compassion is to recognize the two separate voices in your head: the one that works against you and the one that's on your side. That inner ally might be on mute right now; if you want to feel better, not just about the comparisons you make but about yourself as a whole, you can turn its volume up again and again. The more you listen to it, the stronger it gets, and the louder it becomes. Think of your mind like a radio. One station screams judgement and fear. The other plays calm, truth and strength. The dial is in your hands. Choose the station that has your back. The voice you choose to listen to will shape the way you experience yourself. So, make sure the loudest one is the one that supports you. Whenever the voice of that critic strikes, use your answer to this question so you are actively engaging your self-compassionate voice: 'What is the compassion I need right now?' This question is your cue to activate your inner ally, not later, but in the very moment you feel like turning against yourself.

Below are some examples of the two inner voices to help you recognize them in your own thoughts, so you can shift away from the one that criticizes you and move towards a more compassionate and understanding way of seeing yourself.

Inner Critic: 'You're just not good enough. You never will be. There's perfect people and there's you, you're so broken. There's something so wrong with you.'

Self-Compassion: 'Listen, no one is perfect, not even the people who seem like they are. They just hide their struggles better. You're not broken. You're human. And when things are hard, that's when you need kindness the most, especially from yourself.'

Inner Critic: 'You make so many mistakes, you're constantly messing up.'

Self-Compassion: 'Mistakes don't mean failure, they mean you're trying something. And trying means you're brave, and you're growing. Look at everything you've already done. You're so much stronger than you think, and no mistake can erase that.'

Inner Critic: 'Look at you. Your life's such a mess. Everyone else has it together and you're still stuck. What's wrong with you?'

Self-Compassion: 'I know it feels that way, but you're not a mess, you're just figuring things out. And you're doing your best, which is more than enough. No one has it all together, no matter how it looks.'

7. Focusing on gratitude instead of others

Gratitude can be surprisingly powerful when it comes to self-comparison, but only if you're using it in a way that actually helps you. It works by retraining your mind to focus on what's present, not what's missing. The more you tune into your own experiences, progress and achievements, the less time you spend fixating on what everyone else is doing. Gratitude does more than just pull you away from unhealthy comparison, it can also change how you see yourself. When you make it a regular habit, it can help rewire your brain to notice what's already good in your life. And when that happens, the urge to measure yourself against others naturally starts to fade. Say aloud: 'I choose to see the beauty in my life as it is right now.'

Gratitude also helps dismantle a scarcity mindset, which is that nagging belief that success, happiness or love are limited, and if someone else has more, you have less. That kind of thinking fuels self-comparison because it makes every achievement feel like a competition you're losing (or worse, one you've already lost). But if life really worked that way, no one new would ever move forwards, no breakthroughs would happen, and no second chances would exist. Yet they do. Every single day. The truth is, abundance exists. There's always more – more opportunities, more possibilities, and so much more room for you.

That said, not all gratitude is helpful. Like I said at the start, it only works if you're using it in a way that actually helps you. Sometimes people can feel worse when they try to practise gratitude because they do it in a way that reinforces unhealthy comparison. They tell themselves, they should be grateful because other people have it worse, and instead of feeling uplifted they end up feeling guilty. If gratitude worked in that way, psychologists would call it a day by just showing people pictures or videos of those in worse situations, and that would solve your pain. But that's not how it works. The truth is, the sense of inadequacy they were struggling with in the first place is still there, only now it's worse. It's wrapped in guilt and shame, and it whispers, 'You're ungrateful too.'

Gratitude isn't about guilting yourself into feeling better. It's not: 'I should be grateful because other people have less.' It's: 'I am grateful for . . . FULL STOP' without comparison. Gratitude is also something you can't force. Gratitude is a feeling, and feelings can't be demanded into existence. If you try to force it, it can become another thing you're failing at. And that turns something that's supposed to be healing into another form of self-judgement. True gratitude is about noticing and appreciating the good that's already here. And when you practise it that way, it has the power to loosen the grip of unhealthy self-comparison. So, make it a habit to ask yourself every day: 'What am I grateful for?' Hit the pause button and just appreciate what's made you feel good, no matter how big or small, maybe it's:

- The warmth of the sun on your face
- The sound of rain falling
- A deep breath that felt calming
- The comfort of a warm blanket on a cold night
- Laughter with someone you love
- The feeling of standing tall
- The quiet triumph of making it through another hard day
- The beauty of a sunrise
- The peace of a slow morning
- The love inside you – some of which, you're learning to give to yourself

Things to hold onto . . .

Self-comparison is like an invisible ruler you use to measure our worth and value against everyone else's. And it's a completely natural tendency – we all do it. It's like a mental program running quietly in the background for most of us.

When self-comparison becomes unhealthy it shakes your confidence, keeps old wounds alive and leaves you stuck in that sense of not being good enough.

Healthy self-comparison is about seeing something in someone else that sparks something in you. It nudges you towards growth, inspiration or positive action. It gets you out of your comfort zone, energizes you and motivates you to do new things.

Healthy comparison happens through the lens of your own values. Setting boundaries around the kinds of comparisons you make. Noticing envy and learning how to turn it into something useful. Choosing compassion over criticism. And shifting your focus towards gratitude instead of getting caught up in what others are doing.

Part Nine

Protecting Yourself from Toxic Behaviour

Toxic behaviour hurts. And it's a basic human right to protect yourself from anything that harms you. Toxic behaviour is any action from someone that chips away at your well-being. It disrespects you, belittles you, crosses your boundaries and leaves you questioning your worth. At its heart, it's self-serving; it's about someone using their power or influence over you to get what they want, regardless of how it affects you. Toxic behaviour doesn't belong to just one kind of relationship, it can happen anywhere. It shows up in romantic relationships, friendships, families, workplaces, schools, universities, online and in your community.

Toxic behaviour also takes many forms. In this part of the book we're going to name those behaviours. I'll help you recognize them for what they are, understand why people do them, and most importantly, give you practical tools for handling them when they show up in your life.

This part of the book is about awareness. It's about seeing clearly. Because one of the toughest things about toxic behaviour is that it often hides behind words that sound caring, but actions can tell a very different story. Real care doesn't leave you confused. Real care doesn't manipulate or control. Real care shows up in actions that match words, again and again, not just when it's convenient. If you've been on the receiving end of the kinds of behaviours we're about to explore, you've probably already felt that gap between what someone says and how they actually treat you. One of the most common threads running through all toxic behaviour is emotional manipulation. It pulls you in, creates confusion and makes you question yourself. It casts an emotional fog, making it hard to see your way out – especially when you've drifted there slowly. That's how people who use these behaviours operate. They don't strike with full force from the start, because you'd notice, and you'd step back. Instead, it starts small and subtle, creeping in bit by bit. By the time you realize something feels wrong, you're already in deep, second-guessing yourself. The more you understand these patterns – why people act in these ways, how it plays out and what it looks like – the more that fog begins to lift.

This part of the book is about protecting yourself, about seeing things as they really are, not as you wish they were. And it's about making a quiet, steady commitment to stop arguing with the reality you see. You've already done a lot of work in this book. As we move through this part of the book, I want you to hold onto to your values, they're your anchor. Use them to check in with yourself by asking yourself: 'Does the way someone treats me, or the way I've been taught to let them treat me line up with what I value for myself and the life I want to live?' And if it doesn't you don't have to allow it. You can use everything you've learned so far about boundaries, being assertive, handling conflict, processing emotions, along with what I'll share in this section, to change that. Using all these tools will help you stand a little taller, and make sure you're taking care of yourself when it matters most.

Chapter 1:
The Gut-Punch Moment

Have you ever had someone say or do something to you that left you feeling shocked to your core, like a punch to the gut? That strong somatic response can be a powerful red flag. It's often the moment something in you snaps awake and realizes this isn't right. In healthy relationships, there's trust and predictability. You know where you stand, even when things get tough. But psychologically unhealthy people can be unpredictable. One minute they're kind – and the next, they're someone else entirely. That sudden shift can shake you deeply. It rattles your sense of safety, your trust, and you no longer feel grounded. The gut-punch feeling is a common, visceral, almost physical response to emotional shock. The sudden perception of unsafety comes not just from what they said or did – but from the jarring contrast between the person you thought you knew and the stranger now standing in front of you. When someone behaves unpredictably like this, it can trigger a stress response in your body. You feel anxious, on edge, thrown off balance, because your nervous system is trying to protect you in a situation that suddenly doesn't feel safe any more, and nor does it make sense.

That deep unsettling feeling tells you that the other person has the capacity and the willingness to push you so far that it creates such an intense reaction within you. And then, just as quickly as they've caused you the shock, they can switch back to 'normal' like nothing has happened. This leaves you confused, wondering what to expect next, and hoping that this shock was just a one-time thing. But here's the thing, that gut-punch feeling will show up again, whenever you're treated that way.

So remember what it feels like, and listen to it. It's your body's warning system. That visceral reaction is your internal alarm, telling you that your emotional safety has been violated.

Chapter 2:
Why Do They Do It?

People engage in toxic behaviour because it gets results; it gives them control, attention or the outcome they want, regardless of the harm it causes. As we go through each behaviour, you'll see what they're trying to get out of it. Many people who behave in these ways have their own issues. These could be personality disturbances, where they have a disregard for other people's rights and feelings, and a deep lack of empathy. This can make them self-serving, exploitative and harmful towards others. They may have suffered past trauma, which has affected their emotional development and made it hard for them to form healthy relationships. They can be aware of these struggles, which can leave them feeling insecure and low in self-esteem. Those deep-rooted cracks can create a need to control others; it's an attempt to patch the parts of themselves that feel broken. It makes them feel powerful, while also getting them what they want.

Some people pick up toxic behaviours by seeing them modelled around them. If they grew up in a home where unkind or toxic behaviour was common or even normalized, it becomes second nature for them. Sometimes people point to mental health issues as the reason for their behaviour. And while certain mental health struggles can affect how someone behaves, they don't cause someone to consistently act in toxic and harmful ways. It's also important to know that people who behave in toxic ways will sometimes weaponize mental health diagnoses. When you challenge them on their behaviour, suddenly they say: 'It's because of my trauma' or 'It's because of my depression.' They might even drop a mental health diagnosis you've never heard of, right in the middle of being confronted about their behaviour – as a way to avoid taking responsibility.

Sometimes, people will say, 'I was stressed.' While stress can affect how someone behaves, it's usually only a mild to moderate change. It also tends to be situational, causing only temporary changes in behaviour. It's a one-off, occasional occurrence, and there's typically a healthy apology, explanation and attempt at reparation afterwards. This is worlds apart from someone who uses stress as a shield for repeated cruelty.

Another reason they do it is because it works. It's worked before with other people, and that reinforcement tells them manipulation gets results. There might have been people who have either tolerated it or enabled it, which also makes them think it's okay to keep going.

As tempting as it may be to figure out a definitive reason behind someone's actions, it's less important than the impact their behaviour has on you. I don't think it helps to get lost trying to figure out exactly why they're behaving this way. You'd have to rely on them to be honest, and if someone's acting toxic, that's a pretty clear sign they're not going to be forthcoming with the truth. So focus on how their behaviour affects you, how it makes you feel. That's what really matters. There may be reasons behind it, but never let that excuse their actions, or mistreatment of you.

Chapter 3: Do They Know They're Doing It?

A question I often get asked is, 'Do they know what they're doing?' The answer isn't always simple, but most of the time, yes, they absolutely do. They know exactly what they're doing, they know how to do it and in their mind, their manipulative behaviour isn't just justified, it's necessary. They see you as the problem because you won't fall in line or do what they want; you're 'difficult' in their eyes. So they turn to manipulation as a way to get you to bend to their will.

One of the clearest signs that someone is manipulative is how differently they act when others are watching versus when they're alone with you. If they're kind, charming, composed or even just well behaved in public, but cruel or unpleasant in private, it's a sign they can switch off their bad behaviour when others are watching. That's not proof that the good side is the real version of them, it's proof that they know what's acceptable and are choosing when to show it. If their behaviour makes you question who they really are, remember: the niceness you see around others doesn't erase the harm they've caused you in private. It shows that they're deliberate, and that their actions are working exactly as intended.

People who behave in these ways don't doubt the morality or the impact of their actions on you. They know their behaviour affects you, that's the whole point. They want you to feel a certain way, so you'll do what they want. They don't care about the level of impact on you. What matters more to them is their own feelings and getting their needs met, regardless of the cost to you. The doubts they might have are usually about their ability to manipulate effectively. They might have concerns about whether it's working or if they're getting the reaction they want.

You can ask someone a couple of simple questions to get a sense of how someone sees themselves. For example, when they say or do something that feels off, you can ask, 'Do you think you could be wrong about this?' or 'Do you think there's another way to see this?' And also a more general question: 'Do you ever doubt yourself?' If they say no to any of these, that's a big red flag. Most healthy people can admit when they're wrong or when they experience self-doubt. If someone consistently struggles with this, it can be a sign of an inflated sense of self-importance or difficulty taking accountability, patterns often seen in people who use manipulative or toxic behaviour.

That said, also be cautious if they say 'yes, but' or offer an evasive answer. This shows they're not fully owning up to it; they know that admitting fault outright will make them look bad. So they give you this partial answer instead, which lacks authenticity. It's a way of covering it up while still holding onto some sense of control. Being wrong would threaten their sense of superiority, but so would being caught out, and for someone who behaves in these ways, keeping the upper hand is everything.

Chapter 4:
Is It Them, Or Is It Me?

It's natural to question, is it me? It's a good question to ask yourself, it shows you are self-reflective and that is healthy. Psychologically unhealthy people rarely do that. But just because you're asking the question, and just because they're telling you it's you, and planting doubt and blame, it doesn't mean the answer is yes. Toxic behaviour is designed to make you question yourself, by twisting things until you start to believe you're the problem. Toxic behaviour also involves using anything against you – your personality, your mistakes and your past if it's been difficult. It all becomes something to weaponize. In fact, if you've had a difficult past, people can sometimes pick up on that and that's exactly why certain people might target you. So be mindful of how quickly you share your difficult past experiences with others, especially those where you were mistreated. Opening up too soon, before trust has been proven, can leave you vulnerable to harm. Especially if you're dealing with someone who doesn't have good intentions. These people can misuse the information you give them; they can use your past as a roadmap for how to hurt you. It tells them what you might put up with or what they can get away with, based on how others have treated you before. It also gives them ammunition to use against you later. Unhealthy people will often weaponize what you tell them for their benefit – whether that's to control you, gaslight you or exploit you in other ways. Information about your past is deeply personal; it's about your vulnerability and it deserves to be protected. Not only that, but you don't need to use your pain as proof of anything. Until someone has shown you, through consistent actions, that they're safe and trustworthy, keep your boundaries in place.

If you have been through hard things in the past, you might be more vulnerable to believing it's you that's the problem. But here's what I want you to remember: ***your past doesn't cloud your judgement, it sharpens it.*** It teaches you what feels off, what feels unsafe or unkind, and often this can be felt physically in the body. When something happening now echoes a hurtful experience from the past, it can be your body and mind sending signals to warn you; your past shows you what feels off or unsafe. Having vulnerabilities doesn't make you the problem. It means that if someone is going to be close to you, they need to be the kind of person who has compassion for those parts of you, not use them against you. Being hurt before doesn't mean you deserve less care or kindness. It means you deserve more, and you deserve to be met with care, and behaviour that makes you feel extra safe.

Remember you are not the child any more. You are not the younger or vulnerable version of yourself who was once hurt by someone – the person who cried and was dismissed, uncared for, or ignored. You're an adult now, with power and choice. You are the boss of you – not anybody else. You can listen to that inner voice from the time you were hurt. That voice is the part of you that protects you, it's your boundaries, your learned intuition, your emotional memory of what has already happened. Trauma and past negative experiences often sensitize you to warning signs about unsafe or unhealthy situations. It's like a voice that alerts you when something feels off, reminds you of what you've survived – and also reminds you that you never want to feel that way again. It helps you stay away from people who leave you feeling unsafe, small or shaken, and move towards people who feel safe – people who treat you with care, who make you feel like yourself: calm, steady, happy and free.

Chapter 5:
The Toxic Behaviours

In this chapter, we'll go through ten different types of toxic behaviours. When you recognize these dynamics, it becomes easier to protect yourself from them. You'll also get insight into what benefits these behaviours bring to the person who's using them. As you read through these, keep in mind that, despite the examples of relationships portrayed, these behaviours can show up in all kinds of contexts – friendships, romantic relationships, families, work and more. Another thing to remember is that people who show toxic behaviours rarely have just one, there's usually a mix of them. With each behaviour, you'll find actions that help you protect yourself.

1. Gaslighting

Gaslighting is a word we've all heard, and it's a specific type of psychological abuse that happens in close relationships.[31] The word originates from the 1938 stage play *Gas Light* by Patrick Hamilton. It tells the story of a husband who makes his wife question her own reality, by dimming the gas lights in their home, and then denying it looks different when she notices it. This makes her doubt her perceptions. The play was later adapted into a film about gaslighting, and led to the coining of the term gaslighting. The word gained so much momentum in recent years that, in 2022, Merriam-Webster named it word of the year, defining it as psychological manipulation of a person, usually over an extended period of time, that causes the victim to question the validity of their own thoughts.

Gaslighting is a repeated pattern of behaviour that slowly chips away at your perception, memory and experience of events. It creates confusion and slowly undermines your confidence, and chips away at your ability to believe your own judgement. Gaslighting can take so many forms. And often, it doesn't look obvious at first. Sometimes it's only afterwards, when you're left feeling unsettled or confused, that you start to realize what has happened. In real life, it can show up in all kinds of ways. Sometimes it looks like someone doing or saying something hurtful, and then acting completely normally afterwards. If they seem fine while you're upset or shaken, it can make you question yourself. 'Maybe I'm overreacting. Maybe it wasn't that bad.'

It can also look like ending a friendship because of how someone treated you, and then having them turn around and blame you for the fallout. Maybe they even accuse you of something absurd that never happened, like stealing, lying, whatever – anything to rewrite the story. It can look like someone shouting at you, and when you ask them not to shout, they tell you you're the one who's shouting (this is also a classic projection tactic). It can be asking someone why they seem upset: 'Is everything okay, are you okay?' Instead of answering, they accuse you of being angry or difficult, even when you know you weren't.

They behave badly, and when you call them out, they deny their behaviour, over and over. If they admit to anything, they will twist the story into a much softer, nicer and more palatable version of what happened. They might tell you your mind is playing tricks on you, or, if you have any mental health struggles, blame that for your perception being skewed. It's all to avoid responsibility while making you doubt your own reality. It happens in families too. One parent might treat the children badly, and then turn to the other parent, the one who's been steady and kind, and say, 'I'll never forgive you for the way you treat the children.' Gaslighting is about flipping reality upside down. It is often contradictory, like someone telling you that you're the problem, you're crazy, and then in the next breath saying, 'I'm here to support you, I'd never judge you, I just want to help.' With judgement and concern arriving side by side like that, it scrambles your sense of reality.

There are other common tactics too, like hiding your things. Being told you're too sensitive. Being told you're overreacting. This can make you wonder if your feelings are valid. The truth is it's human to feel hurt when someone's words or behaviour cross a line. That's not being too sensitive, it's being alive to your experience. Feelings just are, they tell you what matters and what's happening. Nobody should tell you you're not allowed to feel what you feel. Anyone who tries to take that away from you is also gaslighting you. Some people who exhibit toxic behaviour, once they learn the word gaslighting, will start using it back at you; weaponizing it in response to you naming something hurtful they've done, they'll shut you down by saying, 'You're gaslighting me.' This is just another form of gaslighting, a classic reversal tactic also used to avoid taking any responsibility.

A person who isn't gaslighting wouldn't respond in such a way. They'd be open to engaging with you, not reacting defensively. They'd care about your feelings and want to understand your perspective. They'd ask you to tell your side, really listen and accept your emotions. And they'd offer an apology. Can you see the difference? One is open, one is defensive. One comes with empathy, the other with invalidation. One takes responsibility, the other shifts the blame. One is genuine communication, the other is blocking you out, shutting you down.

Try to look at the intention behind the response, whether it's rooted in empathy and connection or in trying to avoid it.

Now you have this detailed description of what gaslighting is, the next step is to think about is what you want to do about it. The right approach really depends on your situation. Keep in mind that gaslighters usually won't admit fault or reflect on their behaviour. Challenging a gaslighter about what happened is emotionally draining and, honestly, pretty pointless. Gaslighters feed on attention and reaction, so by calling them out you show them they have control over you, their gaslighting has rattled you, which is what they want. It will usually leave you feeling even more confused and frustrated. The fact that they're gaslighting you already tells you they will dismiss anything you say. Some gaslighters know exactly what they're doing, and others are so invested in their distorted version of reality that they genuinely believe it. Either way, it makes a calm, rational conversation impossible.

That said, you can name the behaviour to them if you really want to. Not because it will change them or lead to an acceptable admission – it won't – but because it might help you. It can be a way of saying, 'I see what's happening here. I'm not confused, and I'm not accepting it.' But be prepared, because what will usually happen when you do this is they'll try to crush you again with more gaslighting. That's their pattern. If you decide to say it, be ready for that. If you do want to name the behaviour, you don't have to use the word 'gaslighting'. You can describe what's happening in your own words, for example, 'I feel like you're trying to make me doubt my own judgement,' or whatever fits your situation. Using your own words can feel safer and carry less risk of triggering more gaslighting. You could also consider doing it in writing, and then setting a firm boundary to ignore whatever comes next from them. It's likely they will send long diatribes, walls of text designed to pull you back in or defend their position; try not to get drawn in. You've made your observations and you've stated your position. You don't need to explain anything more.

You might decide it's better not to engage at all, and that's often the wisest choice. You can still name what happened to yourself. Say, for example: they gaslighted me by doing XYZ, and I won't be treated like that. Or write it down in a journal. This helps you stay clear in your own mind about what happened. It keeps you anchored in your reality when someone has tried to twist it. Be factual, be clear and write it as plainly as you can. And if you ever start to question yourself again, you can go back and read your own words. You can remind yourself: *I know what happened. I trust what I saw. I trust what I felt, I trust my experience*. Sometimes that in itself is the most powerful thing you can do.

Beyond that, if you can, the healthiest thing is to limit contact, or cut it off altogether. That's what really protects you, by taking away their ability to keep twisting things and getting into your head. But if you do have to stay in contact, maybe because of family connections, co-parenting or work, keep everything brief, and in writing. Writing helps protect you and helps protect the truth. Keep your communication factual and as boring as possible. No emotion, no extra details. Nothing for them to twist or use against you later. This is not about being cold, it's about being clear.

Dealing with gaslighters is emotionally and physically draining. It can leave you feeling raw, and wounded. And that's exactly why revisiting your boundaries and taking care of yourself in the ways you need to is so important. It's not your fault that you were hurt in these ways, but it is your job to take care of the part of you that's been hurt. Whether it's rest, an activity or something else soothing, do what you need to do to look after yourself.

2. Projection

Projection is when someone accuses another person of behaviours or traits that actually describe themselves. The best way to understand it is to imagine your own internal world – your thoughts, feelings, insecurities, behaviours – and then take something you don't like, or can't handle about yourself, and 'see' it strongly in someone else. It's a defence mechanism that protects the person doing it from facing uncomfortable truths about themselves. For example, a person might accuse someone else of having angry outbursts, when it's actually the accuser who behaves that way. Another example is one seen in high-conflict divorces, where one parent accuses the other of brainwashing the children to turn them against the other parent – but it's the accusing parent who's been doing the brainwashing all along.

Here's another example: Nikita and Mason. Mason is emotionally volatile, out of control and cannot regulate his feelings. He knows this about himself, but instead of acknowledging and accepting that he is emotionally unstable and getting help to learn how to regulate his emotions better, he accuses Nikita of being like this. He's projecting his internal chaos onto her. Because he's so ashamed of his own heavy, uncomfortable feelings, it feels too painful for him to face them; if he projects them onto her, it allows him to focus on her problems, diverting the attention away from his unresolved issues. It's his way of saying, 'look at how damaged you are', without ever having to confront his own wounds.

People who project like this usually have a very fragile sense of self and they want to maintain a superior image without any flaws. They find it deeply threatening to accept that, like everyone else, they also have some negative characteristics, and that's why projection becomes their go-to toxic behaviour. Projection is a powerful way to deflect blame, avoid self-reflection, and maintain a distorted sense of self and reality – while also breaking down someone else's confidence, making them easier to control.

Just like gaslighting, confronting the person doing the projection rarely works. It's futile trying to convince them that they're projecting. They are so emotionally invested in their projection that they will not be open to reason at all. Often the best way to deal with it is to recognize that it's happening. Ask yourself: *'Is what they're accusing me of out of sync with how I know I am as a person? Is it how other people see me? Is it consistent with what people who care about me say to me?'* Then firmly and calmly state your reality to yourself, because what matters most is what you think of yourself, and being steady in your own truth.

How much you engage with them will again depend on the context of your relationship, but usually the less engagement you have with people like this, the better. If you do want to, or have to, say anything to them, you can assert a boundary like: 'I understand that's what you think, but I'm not feeling angry right now' and then walk away. Or you can say: 'I'm willing to talk about XYZ, but I won't engage in conversation while you keep making accusations.' It's important that you don't get drawn into a relentless back and forth. That's why I suggest low engagement. Notice what's happening, name it, set your boundary and move on.

3. Blame-shifting

Blame-shifting is a toxic behaviour where someone avoids taking responsibility for their own actions by placing blame onto someone else. Blame-shifting is often used to manipulate people for personal gain. At the same time, it's a shield that protects the person's fragile self-image and helps them avoid accountability.[32] Shifting the blame for things onto somebody else prevents any meaningful discussion of that person's own role in whatever the problem is. For example, with Eric and Nikki, every time there was a problem or a disagreement in their relationship caused by his actions, Eric would say, 'I didn't do anything wrong, it's to do with your past, it makes you sensitive and see me as doing wrong even when I'm not.' Nikki had a difficult childhood, and Eric would weaponize it every time he needed to blame-shift. She said to me, 'I don't understand why he acts like every issue between us is somehow about my past, not about him or what's actually happening now.' The truth is, Eric doesn't believe it himself, he's just using it to avoid taking responsibility. By blaming her, he doesn't have to look at his own choices or admit that he doesn't want to treat her well. This example is especially cruel because Eric drags Nikki's past trauma into the present, turning it into a reason for her upset over his current behaviour.

Dealing with someone who blame-shifts is about recognizing what's happening and understanding that it's not about you. You'll notice when it's happening because the other person will immediately shift the spotlight onto something else they can blame you for.

Just like with other toxic behaviours, a person who uses blame-shifting usually won't acknowledge that they're doing it, nor will they be able to have a reasonable discussion about it. However, if you want to raise it, you could try a phrase like, 'Regardless of what you're saying about me, I'm still upset because you did XYZ.' You could also focus on how their actions made you feel by saying, 'I felt hurt or sad when you did XYZ.' You may also need to set a firm boundary by saying that this behaviour is unacceptable, and you won't continue being blamed in these ways. You can protect yourself by recognizing their attempts for what they are and distancing yourself from them. That might mean keeping interactions brief, stepping back a little or, in some situations, ending contact altogether. These choices aren't always easy, but they're often vital for your emotional safety.

4. Playing hot and cold

Playing hot and cold is when someone is warm and affectionate one minute – they're kind, thoughtful, make you feel special – and then, out of nowhere, they become cold, distant or off, almost like the positive connection you felt was imagined. And it's not random at all. Nor is it just 'bad communication'. It's often a control tactic, designed to keep you emotionally dependent on them, because how they treat you controls how you feel – that's where their power and control lies.

At first, the hot phase feels amazing. It's compliments, connection, attention, kindness – whatever version of care means the most to you, that's what they'll give you. They might be a friend, they might be a partner, they might feel like a soulmate – but whoever they are, what you have with them feels rare. And in the hot phase, it feels so safe. When someone shows you that much warmth and you feel safe, it's natural to let your guard down. You trust them, so you share more of yourself, your secrets and your vulnerabilities. You start to believe you're building something special and real.

And then, just like that, without warning, they switch it off, and the cold phase starts. It feels brutal because it doesn't come with an explanation. They pull back, they are distant, different, even unrecognizable from what you knew of them.

They might become critical or irritated with you. And when you ask what's wrong, they'll usually say: 'Nothing, I'm fine.' They'll imply everything's normal while you're left spinning, trying to figure out what on earth is happening. This confusion is the whole point. It's what keeps you hooked. You start replaying things in your mind, wondering what you said, what you did wrong, what you need to fix. You work harder for their approval, because you're human and you want to solve the issue. And you want to get back to the place where you felt safe and things were good.

But here's the trap: as soon as you adjust to the cold phase, they'll turn the heat back on. They'll be kind again, attentive and everything will feel back to normal. And just when you start to feel stable, they'll pull away again. This is what's known as intermittent reinforcement, and it's incredibly powerful. It's what creates trauma bonds. It hooks you on the hope that the good version of them is coming back soon – if you just try hard enough, or if you're patient enough, or if you stop being 'too sensitive' and don't put a foot wrong, please them in every which way you can think of, it'll be okay again. But the truth is that none of this is about what you did or didn't do. Their behaviour has nothing to do with your worth. It's a reflection of their need for control.

If during the cold phase, they sense you're pulling away, they notice you're getting your independence back, that you've accepted whatever it was it's over with them, so you're detaching, they'll suddenly flip the switch. They're back, with warmth, sweetness, care and attention. Saying all the right things. It's like they can sense your independence creeping in and they know they're losing their grip on you. So they rush in with a flood of kind gestures, and all the things you've been craving, and it's not because they've changed but because they're trying to pull you back in. After all the distance and silence it feels like such a relief. It's tempting to believe maybe this time it's real and it will last. But it's not a real change. The warmth is just a way to maintain control, a brief return to the 'hot' phase that lasts long enough to pull you back in, so they feel like they've got you exactly where they want you. And every time you get caught in that loop, it takes something from you. Another layer of your confidence, a layer of the trust you have in yourself, and some of your peace. It wears you down without you even noticing, until one day you feel like a shell of the person you were before it all started. And the longer you stay in it, the harder it is to see clearly, because you're living in their emotional weather system. It's sunshine one moment, a storm the next, and you never know what kind of day you're going to have.

Recognizing what's happening is the first step. Stand back and look at the pattern. Write it down if you need to, with dates, so you can clearly see the cycling between hot and cold. Once you do, it gets easier to step out of the loop. Resist the urge to chase them during the cold phase. I know it's hard. But their withdrawal is not about you. It's about what they're trying to get from you. Remind yourself that this is not love, it's not care – it is toxic behaviour, all aimed at control over you and your feelings. And from there, it's about you working on protecting yourself. Stop expecting consistency from someone who's shown you they don't give it. Turn your focus back to your own life, reconnect with your values, with what you need, the things that bring you joy; reset your routines and get back in touch with your friends and family if you've lost contact.

And most of all – don't ever forget this – you don't have to earn consistent respect. It's the bare minimum in any healthy relationship. People who really care about you never want to leave you guessing; real connection doesn't keep you on a string like that. Genuine, healthy connections don't start with a fast, super-intense beginning where everything feels perfect. If you ever meet someone like that, put on the brakes to see what happens. If they have bad intentions and can't sweep you up into their whirlwind, they'll disappear; this can show you that their interest in you wasn't genuine. You deserve better. Walking away from this kind of behaviour isn't a loss, it's reclaiming your peace. It's choosing yourself so you can rebuild what they tried to take from you, and that's your power move.

5. Triangulation

Triangulation – like a triangle – has three parts. There's you (person A), the person who's manipulating you (person B) and a third person (person C). Here's how it works: person B, the manipulator, creates a dynamic where it's them and person C on one side, and you on the other. Person C might be physically present or they might not, sometimes it's just their words or opinions being used against you. The triangle looks like this: person B raises something with you, and they don't like your response. So instead of working it out with you directly and in a healthy way, they go to person C and talk about you in a negative or biased way. They try to pull person C into their version of events, get them to take their side, and then present that united front back to you. People who triangulate do this to create division, to isolate you and to position themselves as the one in control. They want to be right, to control the story, and if they can make you feel outnumbered you might admit you're wrong, and that gives them control over you.

Person C is chosen very carefully. It has to be someone who's going to validate the manipulator's perspective, someone who will agree with whatever they're accusing you of. The whole point is to make you feel outnumbered and to make you think that you must be in the wrong. Because now it's not just them saying it, they've got backup. Person C becomes the vessel the manipulator uses to prove their point. Sometimes person C knows what's happening, but often they don't. Either way, they're being used, by being drawn into a dynamic designed to create confusion, anxiety, jealousy, resentment or even just to punish you. And it often works, because suddenly it's not a conversation between two people any more. It's a triangle, and you're standing in it alone.

Let's look at some examples. Someone accuses you of always moaning and complaining, and you know that you don't. What they're calling moaning is really just you making reasonable requests or expressing your needs, but they don't like that you're doing this. So they label it as complaining. Then they bring a third person in to back them up on this claim.

Another way they might triangulate you is through hearsay. They'll say things like, 'Remember last week when your mum said you're always moaning and complaining? And the other day your friend said it too? People say it to you all the time. Everyone I know who knows you says that about you. It's not me who's the problem, it's you.' They're using other people's voices, real or imagined, to make their perspective feel bigger, heavier and more true.

Another common way to triangulate is by creating jealousy or insecurity. For example, if you're in a relationship, your partner might bring up someone else who's interested in them, dropping comments about how attractive they are, or how much attention they're getting from them. They're using that person to create insecurity, jealousy or competition for your place in their life. It's showing you that there's a threat to your security, and that creates anxiety for you. This might then drive you to behave in ways the manipulator wants, like trying harder to please them, or ignoring when they say something that hurts you. Sometimes it can show up through comparisons with an ex – your partner might describe their ex as easygoing, kind or better in some way, while highlighting your so-called flaws. They say things like, 'She never used to do that,' or 'He never acted like you do.' Both of these scenarios are about using a third person to reinforce their position and influence your behaviour, by making you feel outnumbered, anxious or inadequate.

So what can you do about it? Firstly, spot it. The good thing is, it's identifiable, you just need to watch for somebody bringing in a third person. Whether it's verbal or physical, direct or indirect, if someone is positioning another person against you to argue their point, and it's a repeated pattern, it's likely to be triangulation.

If you want, you can call out the triangulation directly. Calmly say something like, 'I've noticed that whenever I don't agree with you, you bring someone else into it. Why is that?' You could also ask, 'Do you think that's healthy?' Or frame it as something you've learned: 'It's called triangulation. It's an unhealthy pattern, and it's better to deal with issues one-on-one.' Be aware, though, that most manipulators use triangulation habitually, so calling it out like this won't necessarily stop the behaviour; it's primarily about asserting your clarity and protecting yourself.

You can also choose not to participate in the triangle, and avoid falling into the trap of defending yourself. You can say something simple like, 'I don't feel comfortable with this.' If you want to call it out, you can directly address it by saying things like, 'I don't remember person C saying that about me, and even if they did, my interactions with them are separate from my interactions with you.' This challenges the validity of the triangulation and dismisses what they're trying to use against you. You can also say, 'That's not how I perceive myself.' Or you can shut the conversation down altogether by saying something like, 'This isn't an issue to involve other people in, I won't take part in that type of conversation.'

As with all toxic behaviours, set firm boundaries for yourself around anyone who triangulates you. These dynamics are unhealthy, and staying involved with someone who uses triangulation can often lead to more confusion and stress.

6. Emotional shape-shifting

Emotional shape-shifting is when someone constantly changes the emotional role they're playing in a conversation. For instance, they might rapidly flip between being the aggressor, the victim and the hero. It's an attempt to manipulate, control the narrative or get a reaction out of you. It's a messy, confusing cycle, and the purpose behind it is to control you through chaos. You never know which version of them you're going to get. One minute they're angry, the next they're playing the victim, and then suddenly they're trying to rescue or help you. It leaves you stuck trying to figure out which version of them you're dealing with, and when you try to respond to one, another pops up. This constant shifting makes it almost impossible to get anywhere near a resolution for whatever triggered the conversation in the first place.

Let's take a look at Mimi and AJ. Mimi makes a request to AJ, he responds by criticizing her. Mimi naturally tries to talk it through, to understand why he's reacting this way. But then, suddenly, AJ flips the script. He goes from criticizing her to telling her, 'I love you, I'm here to support you.' Now, Mimi is caught in a wave of confusion. One minute it's one thing, and the next minute it's something completely different. It started with a simple request from Mimi, but then AJ criticized her, then steered the conversation towards vague issues in their relationship, including questioning her emotional stability. When Mimi is trying to process all this, AJ says something like, 'It's not your fault, it's probably because of how your dad was with you.' He doesn't bring this up with care or affection though. It's a weapon to undermine her even more, while also positioning himself as the helper. Mimi's left spinning, trying to figure out what the real issue is, but before she can get a handle on it, AJ tells her, 'Don't worry, I love you. I care about you a lot. I want to help you.' That's how he keeps her off balance. His constant shifting of topics and emotional energy forces Mimi to keep up, but in doing so, it derails the original issue and prevents any real conversation from happening. The emotional landscape is always changing, and because of that, Mimi has no clear footing.

Dealing with an emotional shape-shifter who uses chaos as a control tactic can be exhausting. It's important to recognize if this behaviour is a repeating pattern, not just an isolated incident. It can help to start journaling the different emotional shapes they shift through, noting the dates and how often it happens. Seeing it all laid out can make the pattern clearer and help you label what's happening, so it's not as easy for them to undermine you.

If you find yourself caught in an emotional shape-shift, resist the urge to chase their emotional tail. That's exactly what they want, to keep you on edge, reacting to every change. Instead, just step back and observe them. Let them change from one thing to the next without jumping in to match their pace. This gives you the distance to see the pattern clearly and figure out how you want to respond, rather than getting caught up in the emotional back-and-forth.

If they're a person that you have to be involved with, and

you want to manage their behaviour differently, you can say something like, 'We were talking about X, can we please go back to that?' If the shape-shifting starts again, just end the conversation. You can then consider moving the conversation to writing instead, so you don't get lost in the chaos of all the avenues they try to pull you down. Prolonged interactions and discussions with an emotional shape-shifter are almost always unproductive; limiting or controlling contact with them is the way to protect yourself.

7. Exploitative attachment

Exploitative attachment is when someone is attached to you, not because they love you or care about you, but because they want continued access to what you can provide. Their attachment is self-serving and conditional on what they receive from you. This might be your presence, your energy, your resources, your money, your status, your practical support. It might be that having you around boosts their social image. It also might be that they just don't like being alone, so they'll keep you attached, even if they don't like or respect you. People like this often see others less as human beings and more as objects or tools to be used for their own benefit. And because they don't want you to know that, they'll give you just enough warmth, just enough kindness to keep you attached, because it serves them.

Because these kinds of people are intense, and the relationship with them is intense, it might feel like love. That's because the attachment can at times feel strong, and all-consuming. But this absolutely isn't love. It's a tether, not a connection. It's parasitic, and it feeds on what you provide. It needs you not for who you are, but for what you give. One of the clearest ways to spot this kind of toxic behaviour is to notice what they take from you, and how rarely they give any of the same back.

Underneath it all they often resent the fact that they need you in these ways. They deeply dislike that they rely on you for anything, so at times they will punish you by treating you poorly. It's a cycle: keeping you close, taking what they want, maintaining control and then punishing you because needing you makes them feel weak.

The only effective way to deal with people like this is distance, separation and walking away. If that doesn't feel immediately possible, get support from people who can help you plan your way out. Tell people you trust what's happening to you – so that you feel supported, so that you're reminded that this isn't a reflection of your worth, it's a reflection of the other person's dysfunction. And, you deserve so much better than this.

8. It's just a joke!

Joking can be a cover for hostility. It's a classic toxic behaviour. It's when someone says something intended to hurt you, undermine you or chip away at your self-esteem, and then when you react, they brush it off as 'just a joke'. It's often used as a cover when people are mocking, criticizing or devaluing you. It tends to pop up when someone says something hurtful and knows you've caught on. They then want you to feel like you're overreacting, so they drop the 'it was just a joke' line to shut you down. This allows them to avoid accountability, and anyone who is watching or listening is left without solid evidence of bad behaviour. Another issue with 'it's just a joke' is that it makes you the problem for not appreciating the humour. While you're left wondering, was it a joke or not? Deep down, you know it wasn't.

The goal of this kind of toxic behaviour is to minimize the impact of their words and deny that they meant anything other than humour. If you challenge them, they might even say, 'How could you think that about me? I was just joking!' This then makes you question yourself, your feelings, your instincts, even your memory. It's a form of gaslighting. But your feelings are your built-in radar. They tell you when something's off, and they're usually right, so trust them.

People who do this often lack empathy, they can be passive-aggressive and envious. Jokes are meant to bring people together, spark shared laughter, social bonding: they create a positive feeling. A joke is something that the majority would typically find funny. If someone labels a statement as a 'joke' but it's not funny to most people, and targets or belittles someone, it functions as a disguised insult rather than genuine humour. Don't let them hide behind the 'it's just a joke' excuse. If you feel comfortable, and you want to, you can tell them it wasn't funny and it hurt your feelings. You can also ask them not to do it again. You don't have to laugh off things that don't feel funny to you. If it becomes a repeated pattern, where their jokes are often at your expense, always cutting, always followed by blame when you react, then it's not humour, it's manipulation. If you're in this situation, it's not just about setting boundaries in the moment, but also stepping back and asking yourself if this person is actually emotionally safe for you to be around? A relationship where you're constantly bracing for the next so-called joke is not a respectful one, especially when you've told them it hurts you, and they continue.

9. The silent treatment

Most of us have experienced the silent treatment at some point. It's that sharp, intentional pulling back when someone goes silent on you to punish you and control you. It can last for hours, days or even weeks. And it's often accompanied by subtle eye-rolling, turning away, looking you up and down, or the cold shrug of a shoulder. All of it is supposed to send you the same message: I'm shutting you out. I'm not happy with you. And I want you to feel it. It's a quiet cruelty that can leave you questioning yourself as you sit in the empty space they've created.

The silence often follows a moment where you did something they didn't approve of – maybe you went out with friends, maybe you spoke up for yourself, maybe you simply made a choice they couldn't control. And then the silence fell to pressure you back into line. It's about getting you to change, back down or stop doing the thing they didn't like. People who use silence this way tend to place their feelings and their needs above yours, as if only their experience matters. Your hurt doesn't move them and what you need doesn't matter to them. The silent treatment can leave you feeling anxious and confused, replaying every moment in your mind, wondering what you did wrong, how to fix it, how to get back into their good books. Because they're not telling you what it is, they are holding all the power. They get to decide when things should go back to normal, and when you've suffered enough. Repeatedly being on the receiving end of the silent treatment can wear you down. It can chip away at your self-worth, leave you walking on eggshells, doubting yourself, and questioning your right to your own feelings and choices.

Not every silence is about control or punishment, and sometimes people do go quiet because they need space. There's a difference between manipulative silence and someone simply needing time to process their thoughts or calm their emotions. Healthy people who do the latter will usually let you know that's what they're doing. They might say something like,

'I'm feeling overwhelmed and I need a bit of time to think about things, so I might be quiet for a bit.' And in their quiet moments, they're not using hostile body language towards you. Their silence doesn't stretch into days or weeks. Nor does it leave you feeling anxious or walking on eggshells. This kind of healthy pause is about emotional regulation, not power or control. Their quiet is just space to settle themselves so they can meet you with care. And when they come back to you, they return with warmth, openness and a willingness to talk things through. They're interested in revisiting whatever happened so you can both understand each other better.

Before you decide how to respond, the first step is to recognize which type of silence you're dealing with. Once you know which one it is, you can decide what to do about it. Sometimes calling out the behaviour can clarify things. Simply saying, 'Are you upset with me? You seem quiet?' But this will often bring the telling response of 'I'm fine,' said in a cold, or passive-aggressive tone. Here, they're showing you something important. They're telling you they don't intend to name the problem. They want you to remain uncertain, anxious and off-balance, and they're okay with treating you like this. In that moment, it's important not to hand over more power by pleading for answers or guessing what you did wrong. That's exactly the dynamic they want – to watch you scramble while they withhold clarity. So ask once, calmly, and leave it there. The next thing to consider is their intent. If their silence is being used to hurt, punish or control you, be honest with yourself about that. A person who regularly uses the silent treatment as a weapon is showing you how willing they are to disrespect and harm you. Because most people who do this are unwilling to communicate in a healthy way, they rarely change that pattern. So it's worth asking yourself whether staying involved with them is good for you.

10. Secret animosity

Secret animosity is a feeling of hidden hostility, resentment or ill will towards somebody. It's when someone has those negative feelings but doesn't openly express them. Instead, they hide their true feelings, appearing friendly or neutral despite harbouring dislike, hatred or opposition towards you. They're often the silent observers of your actions, looking you up, asking others about you, wanting to meet you for updates and even checking your social media through secret burner accounts. Secret animosity is often driven by insecurity, jealousy, envy and resentment, so strong that they fixate on you. They can't just distance themselves, their insecurity keeps them obsessed with you, they want to maintain a relationship so they can keep an eye on you, on what you're doing and, in some cases, benefit from what you're doing.

So, if it's a secret, how can you spot it and what can you do about it? People with secret animosity can slip up because their underlying feelings are too strong to fully hide. This shows up in passive-aggressive behaviour, such as sarcasm or subtle sabotage. They'll disguise criticism as compliments designed to land a jab while giving them plausible deniability. They make subtle digs that aren't too obvious – but just enough to make you feel uncomfortable. And if you pick up on it, they'll often hide behind 'I was just joking' as a way of avoiding being found out. They might also have a tendency of pointing out your flaws or insecurities, disguising them as jokes or as fake concern.

They rarely offer genuine encouragement or support. They won't cheer you on or make an effort to help you succeed. Instead, you might get lukewarm praise, but only when it's expected, like when others are around. Their enthusiasm is always off, it doesn't carry the warmth or energy of someone who genuinely cares. When you compare it to how people who truly support you show up, it feels hollow. They want information about you not because they care about you, but because they want to see where you stand relative to them, or if there's anything they can use to their advantage to feel superior. They're often in covert competition with you, and may be copying you behind your back, trying to get what you have or to outdo you in other ways.

You might also hear them expressing negative thoughts and feelings about other people. They might also gossip and talk negatively behind your back, expressing their animosity to others, which you might even hear about. Another thing to look out for is how you feel when you're with them, how much interest they show in your feelings, how genuine and reciprocal the connection feels. Just like with other toxic behaviours, dealing with secret animosity is about paying attention to patterns of behaviour. If you notice any patterns, you might have the natural desire to confront the person, especially since their frequent interest in you might have led you to believe you're close, and in close relationships we often believe we can have these kinds of conversations. But people who harbour hidden hostility and resentment don't usually admit to it. Instead, they deny it, defend themselves or distance themselves from you to avoid confrontation. A more effective approach is to set firm boundaries. Distance yourself, spend less time with them and share less with them. If they don't genuinely care about you and are willing to be two-faced, they don't deserve a place in your life.

Chapter 6:
The Second-Chance Checklist

Many people wonder whether it's worth giving someone who's hurt them a second chance. They want to believe that change is always possible, and sometimes it is. But usually, when it comes to deeply ingrained toxic behaviours, change is rare, and if it does happen, it's neither quick nor easy. If you want to give someone a second chance first reflect on the reasons why you want to. Don't accept less because you feel impatient or desperate to keep someone in your life. Don't let that be the reason you settle for a relationship that doesn't meet your standards. Being treated the way you want and deserve is more important than staying in a relationship or friendship just for the sake of being in it. Waiting for the right person is less painful than suffering through a long, toxic relationship. If you do want to consider giving someone a second chance, it's their patterns of behaviour that you need to focus on most. Giving someone a second chance isn't something to do lightly. If you're considering it, you need to approach it with caution, clear boundaries and a careful look at whether their actions already show real change. Here's some things to look for:

1. They take full responsibility and accountability for their actions – without excuses, deflection or blaming you or others. There should be no 'Yes, I did, but . . .' statements. These are clear signs that they're not

taking full accountability. What you do want to hear is something like: 'Yes, I did XYZ.' Full stop.

2. They show sincere remorse and regret by apologizing, recognizing the harm they caused you, and being willing to talk about it. You don't need to thrash it out endlessly, but there should be an openness and a readiness to engage.

3. Their behaviour actually changes – and that change is sustained and consistent, not temporary. This is about them actively doing the work to rebuild the trust that was broken. You should see a clear shift – in how they speak, act and show up to you. Their words and actions should consistently match. Changes shouldn't be used as a token or credit to excuse future bad behaviour. They don't get to say, 'I haven't done that in a long time' or 'The last time we argued was ages ago', as a way to dismiss new issues.

4. The sharing of power – also look at how power is shared between you now. How do they behave when conflict shows up? Are they still trying to control things, or are they allowing space for you to have a voice and agency? Pay attention to how they respond to any grievances you bring up. Are they defensive? Do they shut you down? Or are they different, open and responsive?

5. Pay attention to how they respond to your feelings. When you say something simple and real like, 'I was stressed yesterday' or 'I felt anxious', how do they respond? Are they interested? Do they show empathy? Do they try to support you?

6. Finally, and most importantly, ask yourself if being treated or 'loved' like this is something you want to endure for the rest of your life. Are you willing to feel like this indefinitely?

Chapter 7: Moving On with Clarity and Compassion

Moving on from toxic behaviour is not simple, so make sure you take care of yourself. What somebody else does to you and the way they treat you is not about you. It's not because you're not worthy, or there's something wrong with you, or that you deserve to be treated badly. It's because of how they are. And their reason doesn't matter, even if it's their trauma. As I said at the outset of this book, just because a person has wounds it doesn't mean they are allowed to bleed onto other people. A healthy person takes responsibility for these wounds and the resulting behaviour that causes harm to others. An unhealthy person doesn't, they don't admit, recognize or accept that they are hurting others, even when others tell them so. Deep down, they know they are, but getting what they want will always take precedence. So, as you move forward, keep your focus on yourself and the things you value. If you've been through any of the toxic behaviours we've explored, treat your experiences with compassion and give yourself what you need – whether that's time, distance, conversation, support from friends or professional help. It's okay to use that support and feel the impact of these behaviours. Take any action you need to help yourself take care of your well-being so you can move on with compassion for yourself. Many of these behaviours cause relational hurt and pain, and in the final part of this book, which is next, we'll look at how you can move past some of that. Take care, and see you there.

Things to hold onto . . .

It's a basic human right to be protected from anything that harms you – including the toxic behaviour of others.

Toxic behaviour is designed to make you doubt yourself.

The way someone treats you is not a reflection of your worth. It's about their inability or unwillingness to act with care and empathy.

Common toxic behaviours include gaslighting, blame-shifting, projection – 'what's inside me, I see in you'– being hot and cold and triangulation, where someone uses another person's words against you to gain control. These can show up in romantic and family relationships, at work and in friendships.

Emotional shape-shifting is where someone constantly changes the emotional role they play, to blind you through confusion and chaos. People who use toxic behaviours often have an exploitative attachment to you.

'It's just a joke', the silent treatment and secret animosity – when someone hides hostility behind a mask of friendliness – are all toxic behaviours that cause harm.

It's vital that you take care of yourself. That might mean creating distance, setting boundaries, focusing on living by your values, seeking support from people you trust, and taking whatever steps you need to move away from harm and begin to heal.

Part Ten

Healing from the Pain Caused by Others

Have you ever been hurt in a way that sticks with you – pain that doesn't seem to fully fade with time, no matter how hard you try? If you have, it's okay to feel like this. Sometimes people hurt us in ways that stay with us for a long time. And even when you think you're moving past it, even when life goes on, that hurt can still be there. Maybe it's not as sharp as it was in the beginning. Maybe it doesn't catch you off guard like it used to, but it lingers. It stays in your thoughts, in your heart and in the way you feel about yourself. This kind of hurt often comes from people we've been close to. People we once trusted and cared about. It can be friends, family, partners, colleagues; everyone has the capacity to hurt us, just like we have the capacity, knowingly or not, to hurt others too.

What feels hurtful is deeply personal. What one individual might brush off without a second thought, another might carry the weight of for years. Because not all pain lands the same way on everyone. Sometimes it's the shock that sticks with you. Other times it's the disbelief and disappointment – that someone you cared about, someone you respected, could treat you like that. And then there's the sadness, the anger, the feeling of betrayal, the confusion and the shame that comes with it. And this kind of pain can leave lasting marks. It can make you doubt yourself, leave you feeling like you don't matter or belong. It can shape how you see relationships. It can make it hard to trust and open up, and hard to feel safe being yourself with people.

I'm not just talking about the obvious hurts, where it's clear someone had the intent to harm you, and those wounds cut deep. I'm also talking about other hurts, the ones where the other person didn't intend to hurt you at all, but you still felt pain. It might be that someone ended a relationship that you didn't want to end. Or when you shared your feelings with someone and they didn't feel the same way about you. Or when a friend pulled away. Or when someone you love chose a path that felt like it left you behind. Sometimes hurt comes from someone making a choice that they're entitled to make, but that choice breaks your heart. This might lead to the pain of limerence – that deep, consuming, almost obsessive longing and pining for someone who just doesn't feel the same way about you.[33]

In this part of the book, we're going to look at the pain that comes from others. Why it can feel so intense, and so long lasting. Why it can make you pine for people who aren't good for you, or who simply aren't coming back to you. And most importantly, how you can begin to heal from all this and move forward – by understanding it, processing what happened, giving it space and finding the right kind of closure.

Chapter 1: Understand the Roots of Your Pain

The first step in healing from hurt is to name what actually happened. You already know who caused it, but it can help to name the kind of experience it actually was. Was it betrayal, rejection or something else? Describing what happened helps untangle it from the jumble of emotions it left behind. After that, we can turn to the feelings it's left you with, how they affect your thoughts and your actions and what you can do to work through it.

There are different types of pain and hurt caused by others, and I've listed some of these below:

> **Betrayal:** When your trust is broken – through infidelity, broken promises or dishonesty, leaving you feeling deceived and disrespected.
>
> **Unreciprocated feelings:** When you share your feelings with someone, but they don't feel the same way, leaving you feeling rejected or unimportant. This can often lead to an unhealthy emotional attachment and longing, which can sometimes develop into limerence.

> **End of a friendship/relationship:** When someone you cared about chooses to end a friendship or relationship you didn't want to lose, leaving you heartbroken and questioning your value.
> **Rejection:** When you feel excluded, abandoned or unwanted by someone you care about, making you feel like you don't matter, it can also lead to limerence.
> **Toxic behaviour:** When someone manipulates or tries to control you, leaving you feeling confused, powerless and emotionally drained.

Take a moment to consider the list above and think about what happened to you. Just take note of it, you don't need to spend ages on this or get every detail right. Just describe the situation in a few sentences if you can. What happened to you? Who the person was? What kind of hurt did they cause you?

Limerence

If your pain is wrapped up in a deep longing for someone who doesn't feel the same, you might be dealing with limerence. This is where you find yourself completely caught up in someone. Thinking about them all the time, even when you don't want to. You get so stuck on them that it takes over everything, you're constantly pining for them, and it feels like it'll never end. Your mind is completely hijacked by the need for them to return your feelings. But the painful truth is, they don't, won't or can't – because they don't feel the way you do. We can't make people feel something they're not naturally going to feel. And a lot of what you're feeling – the sense that they're the perfect person for you – has taken shape in your own mind, possibly shaped by hope, imagination and emotional need. They might not even know the intensity of what you're experiencing. And even if they did, it doesn't mean they'll feel it back. In fact, it might even unnerve them.

Limerence might remind you of the intense emotions of teenage love, when you feel things so overwhelmingly. Limerence might feel like love, but it's not the same. It's your attachment to them that makes them feel like the most special person in the world to you, and makes it feel like love. Love doesn't work like that. And love isn't something you can make someone feel just because it seems like you feel it so strongly. Love is that deep affection, care and attachment that has a two-way street, you both feel that pull towards each other. There's a strong positive bond between you that keeps growing. You both want to be close to each other. And, you come to each other with compassion, empathy and an understanding that's there even without words. The kindness you have for each other is everywhere: in the words you say, the things you do and the time you share together. You want to protect each other from difficult experiences and emotional pain. And your commitment to each other is there, even when the road gets rocky.

So if limerence is behind your pain, the tools we'll explore here apply just as much to that as they do to other kinds of hurt.

Chapter 2:
Process Your Emotions

Regardless of what happened – whether it was a betrayal, unreciprocated feelings, rejection, the end of something you weren't ready to lose, toxic behaviour or being stuck in limerence – the emotions behind your experience need space to be processed. Which means tuning into what the experience has left you feeling. It's gently turning towards the parts of you that are still holding hurt, and giving those feelings space to be felt. That's how healing begins, not by shutting your feelings out but by learning how to sit with them.

When you think back to what the person said or did that hurt you, try to identify the emotions behind it. Instead of just labelling it as hurt, see if you can be more precise. Use the table below to highlight the emotions that stand out the most to you. Pay attention to the ones that linger or keep coming up when you reflect on the situation.

Different Kinds of Emotional Pain

Deceived	Heartbroken
Disrespected	Confused
Rejected	Abandoned
Unimportant	Unwanted

Small	Disappointed
Shocked	Ashamed
Fearful	Embarrassed
Powerless	Frustrated
Angry	Resentful
Sad	Anxious
Betrayed	Insecure
Lonely	Vulnerable
Isolated	Empty
Unseen	Bitter
Guilty	Disillusioned

Once you recognize those emotions, you can use the 'Feel Your Feelings' exercise from p. 69 to process them.

Feeling those emotions every time they show up helps you work through them again and again – letting the heat in them settle, giving your mind space to calm its reactions. Acknowledging your emotions is the opposite of avoiding or suppressing them. Pushing them down doesn't make them disappear. Instead, they get stuck in your mind and body, often lingering and causing you more distress. Whereas actively feeling emotions helps them run their natural course. Emotions are like energy in motion, when you let them be felt, they can move through you and dissipate. If you don't allow that energy to flow, it can stay stuck. When you avoid them, you also miss the message they're trying to deliver, which prevents you from understanding or meeting your deeper needs. By processing your emotions, you can keep meeting the needs those emotions are pointing you to, and that's a fundamental part of healing.

Chapter 3: Taking the Power out of Painful Thoughts

When you've been hurt, certain thoughts can settle in – almost without you realizing, and they can start to play on repeat. It's important to know what those thoughts are, because when they come wrapped in pain, they can sound like truth. And the more they repeat, the more convincing they seem. That's just what the mind does with hurt that hasn't had space to heal, it circles back, again and again. But not every thought is true, even if it feels real because of the very real feelings it comes with. When you can name these thoughts and notice them showing up, there are gentler, truer things you can hold onto instead. Things that help you reframe what's happened and bring balance to how you think about it.

Here are some common thoughts people can carry after being hurt by others, along with some truer, kinder thoughts to hold on to. You can use these as affirmations, say them aloud or repeat them in your mind to reconnect with your strength and your value.

There are also thoughts that go wider than that, thoughts about life and your place in it. When people hurt us, it can plant deep beliefs about how life works. These thoughts can also shape how you move through life – how close you'll get to people, what you expect from them, and from life itself.

When you think . . .	It might help to remember . . .
'I must be such a bad person for them to treat me this way.'	The way someone treats me reflects who they are, not who I am. Being hurt doesn't mean I deserved it. It just means I'm human, and someone chose to be unkind to me.
'If I could just prove I am good enough for them, they might finally want me.'	I don't have to prove anything to be loved. My worth isn't up for debate, persuasion or negotiation – it exists, full and whole, exactly as I am.
'I should've seen it coming. I'm so stupid for trusting them.'	Trusting isn't foolish, it's a sign of courage. It means I was open-hearted. That's not something to shame myself for, it's something to honour.
'No one will ever understand or care about me.'	It can feel like no one will understand when you've been hurt deeply. But there are people who know how to hold others with care. Maybe not these people. But there are others.
'What did I do to deserve this?'	I didn't deserve this. Some people act from their wounds, it has nothing to do with my worth.
'If I wait long enough they'll realize how much I mean to them.'	Holding onto hope keeps me tethered to someone who's already gone. Letting go doesn't erase what our relationship meant to me. It just means I'm choosing peace over uncertainty.
'I'll never be able to trust anyone again.'	Trust might feel far away right now, and that's okay. It will return when safety does.
'There's something wrong with me.'	There's nothing wrong with having needs or feelings. It's human, and there's nothing shameful about that.

'Why can't I just let go?'	Letting go isn't a switch I can flip. It's something that will happen over time, once I've had the space to heal.
'I don't matter. I'm not important.'	I do matter. I have always mattered. Someone else's inability to see that doesn't change the truth of who I am.
'I'm damaged.'	Yes, I've been hurt. But I'm not broken. There's so much good in me. I am a good person.
'I'm not worth loving or respecting.'	Being mistreated doesn't diminish my worth. That's something no one can ever take away.
'I'm not strong enough to deal with this.'	Even when I feel tired and small, I'm showing strength, by just sitting with this pain.
'I'm different because of what happened.'	Pain might change me. But that doesn't mean I'm broken. It means I'm wiser, stronger, softer with myself and more awake to what truly matters now.

Healing is also about noticing these beliefs, which are there because of the pain you've experienced, and gently questioning if they're always true. Are those thoughts really the whole story? What happened to you was real, but it doesn't have to be the only voice you live by. So, when those thoughts surface, try meeting them with something gentler and truer to help reframe what you've taken from the experience.

When you think . . .	It might help to remember . . .
'People can't be trusted.'	Some people aren't safe, that's true. But not everyone is the same. Trust can be found, slowly and carefully.
'Life is unfair.'	Sometimes life *IS* unfair. And yet there can still be goodness, love and joy, even when things hurt.
'Nobody really cares.'	When I feel lonely, It can feel like no one cares. But there are people who care about me, and some I haven't even met yet.
'Everyone will leave eventually.'	Some people do leave. And some will stay. The leaving doesn't erase the love that was real.
'People will always hurt you if you get too close.'	Closeness comes with risk. That's part of being human. But love is also where healing happens, and it can happen safely.
'People are dangerous.'	Some are unsafe. It's wise to be discerning and careful. But not every hand reaches out to harm. Some reach to hold you.

Chapter 4:
Take Back the Wheel

Your painful experiences with people can shape how you show up, how much you try and how deeply you actually engage with your life. It can end up having a say in everything you do. And it might not be the voice you want making your choices. But sometimes, without you even realizing it, it slips into the driver's seat, takes the wheel and steers you off course. When you take a step back and see how much of your life you're letting pain steer, you can choose to take back the wheel. To do this, think about what you do – or don't do – because of what's happened. What are the behaviours that come out of that? Begin noticing them. Write them down if it helps. Then come back to your values – the things that really matter to you. Your values hold you to something solid: they give you meaning and the best direction for who you are and how you want to live. They're your guide for the everyday choices you make. When you look at those behaviours through the lens of your values, ask yourself: 'Is what I'm doing taking me closer to the kind of life I want to live? Or is it pulling me away from what I really want?'

Look at your values and ask yourself in what ways your pain-driven behaviour might be pulling you away from them. Take your top five, or even ten, and think about what things you can do that line up more with who you want to be – and less with pain or hurt, so whatever that person did to you isn't the only thing calling the shots. And then, start doing those things, even if it's small, and even if it's slow to begin with. When you start living in a way that's guided by meaning and purpose, the hurt softens. The pain doesn't grip you so tightly, and you're not stuck in it in the same way.

For instance, if pain has planted the belief, 'I'm not good enough,' how does that shape what you do? Maybe you put yourself down, or you stop trying new things. Maybe you settle for less than you want, or expect nothing at all. Or you might constantly compare yourself to others, looking for proof that you're not enough. You can ask yourself: 'Do these actions reflect what I care about? Are they helping me move towards the kind of life I want to live?' If you value acceptance it includes accepting yourself, and making space for the thought, 'I'm not good enough', without letting it steer the direction you go in. If you value self-compassion, it means speaking to yourself with kindness, especially when things feel tough. If you value courage, it's about showing up even when you're afraid. And valuing respect definitely includes respecting yourself – treating yourself with dignity, especially when you know you want and deserve more.

If limerence is pulling at you, you might find yourself holding back in certain areas of your life, waiting for something to change or for a dream to come true. But that waiting can stop you from living your life the way you want. The pining for that person might not stop right away even when you do other things, and that's okay. But if you sit with just the longing on its own and do nothing else, you're not just carrying that pain – you're also carrying the pain of not moving forward. You're holding yourself in place, waiting for something that may never come, while life passes you by. But if you keep moving forward, even with that longing there, you start to take back control. You do things that matter to you, things that move your life in the direction you want it to go anyway. The pain might still be there, but now it's not being made worse by you holding back.

Chapter 5: What to Do When You Can't Move On

Feeling stuck after being hurt can take over your everything. The pain swirls through your thoughts, drains your energy, leaving you unsure of how you can move forwards. In this chapter, I want to help you make sense of that stuckness. Because more often than not, it's not that you can't move, it's that you don't know how to yet. And without realizing it, you might be doing things that are keeping you right where you are. The tools in this chapter will help you change that so you can find your way out.

This kind of stuckness can come from the heartbreak of a relationship you didn't want to end, the pain of limerence, unreciprocated feelings or rejection – each leaving you devastated, questioning your worth and still longing for that person. It can also come from a friend who pulled away, someone who ghosted you, a person you had a deep attachment to, even if the connection was unhealthy. Or even from unresolved conflict, where you never got to a resolution, so it left you feeling like things are unfinished, that you can't really move on until you get some sort of closure.

If it's heartbreak, you might find yourself wondering what it is about you that they don't like. What went wrong between you? Why didn't they want you the way you wanted them?

And why is this sending you into a spiral of overthinking, dwelling and obsessing over them? You get stuck replaying everything in your mind, revisiting every moment between you and adding in self-blame: 'If only I had done this differently . . . If only I had known that . . .' You run through every possible turning point, imagining how things could have been different if only you had acted a certain way. This is like blaming or punishing yourself, which research shows can worsen things.[34]

The stress, the anxiety, the low mood – it's all there, and it hits so hard when you're craving a response but all you're getting from the person who hurt you is silence. For relief, you might escape into fantasies, imagining how one day everything will work out perfectly between you. Though 'fantasy' might not be the right word, because it's not just a happy daydream; there's a lot of pain in it for you, and often, that pain is something you're dealing with all alone. You might try to ease the pain by doing things like obsessively checking their social media, searching for anything about them online, going through old photos, replaying memories of them or talking about them with others – who might be getting tired of hearing it all. But you'll do anything to keep the dream alive, even if it makes you feel worse. Somewhere in your mind, you still hold the hope that something might change, that they'll make it right, or at least see what they've done wrong to you. Dwelling on these thoughts, imagining the person changing, or coming back, can create false hope. It keeps you tied to the past, caught in the longing. And as long as your focus stays on them, it's not on you. It's not on your healing, so you stay stuck.

You might also push other people away because you're consumed by this one person and the need for things to work out. And it's not just other people – you might find it hard to concentrate and hard to do the things you need to get done. You may even start changing who you are, how you look, how you act – thinking that if you could just be the person you think they want, things might finally change. All of this signals to your mind that this situation is urgent, and that they're important, even vital, to your well-being. So your mind backs you up, encouraging you to focus on them more, by presenting you with more memories and triggers. The more you focus on them in that idealized way, the more valuable they seem in your mind. And the more valuable they seem, the more you want them and their acceptance. And the more you want this, the more you get caught up in trying to make them want you back – trying to earn their acceptance, and care. It becomes a draining spiral, a helter-skelter with no clear end. The further you slip into it, the more lost you become. And the more lost you are, the harder it feels to imagine letting go of them – or even believing that moving on is possible.

Sometimes the longing for them is tied to the idea that if they once cared, how could they hurt you? It doesn't make sense. So the pining and the limerence can become a way to hold onto a version of them that felt good – even when their actions show otherwise. And sometimes it's not even about them at all – it's the positive qualities you have that you've projected onto them. Your brain clings to that image because it's less painful than facing the truth of who they really were. The longer you're stuck in this place, the more it feeds the idealized version of them that exists in your mind – shaped by who you think they could be, if only things had gone differently. If only they'd stayed, or chosen you, or seen what you see. It's the magic you've created in your own head. But that's not the actual person. The real person is the one who said no to you, the one who isn't giving you the response you want, the one who's made it clear they're not interested or available, they're not willing to meet you in the way you want them to. When you hold onto an idealized version of them, you're holding onto something that isn't real – the real version is what they've shown you. You're not seeing them for who they truly are. And that's not because you're being naive or foolish – it's just that when we're hurting, the mind often softens reality to protect us from the full weight of the pain. Especially when it senses the truth might be too hard for us to sit with.

By dismissing reality you're also not accepting their decision, their feelings, or their right to those feelings. Instead, you're elevating your longing and desires above their choices. In a moment, we'll move on to how you start finding your way out of this. Part of that healing is accepting their agency – respecting their right to have their own feelings (just like you allow yourself to have yours) and make their own decisions, even if those decisions hurt you. It's also about not putting your desires above their choices and their free will. And this isn't about blaming you – it's about understanding how your mind can start distorting reality when desire takes over. That's when things can become unhealthy, with you finding yourself in a cycle of obsession that's hard to let go of. Practising acceptance also means accepting that the person you see is who they are – and they're probably not going to change. It's about facing the reality of the hurt, not clinging to the ideal version of them you've built in your head. It's easy to hold onto the hope that they'll change, apologize or that somehow, one day, things will work out. Especially if there were real moments of connection between you. That's what you're trying to get back to. But waiting on something so uncertain (and hurtful) can take up more of your life than you realize, or really want it to. You end up holding space for someone who might never come back in the way you need, and in the meantime your own life is put on pause.

Getting stuck on someone is usually a temporary phase. But it's often maintained by the way you think, how you feel, and how you react to both. And when you don't take action to get out of it, it can go on much longer – the longer it lasts, the more of your life it takes you away from. From the things you care about. One of the fascinating – and painful – things about this kind of fixation is that the person going through it genuinely believes the other person is the solution to their pain. It really feels that way. But they're not, even if every part of you is convinced they are. The real solution is to look at what's driving the fixation itself – to understand where it's coming from, what it's tied to and why it's taken such a strong hold of you. And then gradually working on those things. If you don't, the stuckness with this person might fade, but it may not disappear completely. It can also find someone new to attach to. If you look back, you might already see this is a repeat pattern.

Another sign they're not the solution to your pain is this: if they suddenly became available, and you truly got to know them, your feelings might shift – or even fade. Again, you might already have experienced this with other people in the past. It happens when you start noticing things about them that you don't actually like, because they don't match the wonderful version you'd built up in your mind. That version was shaped by them being unattainable, and their unavailability increased their perceived value, along with all the fantasies you wrapped around that to protect yourself from pain. But once you really get to know them, you see that the story your mind created was far removed from who they actually are. The version that felt so perfect wasn't really them – it was a fantasy built from hope and longing. I can't tell you how many people get to this point and say, 'Ugh, what was I thinking?' And it's not that there's anything wrong with the other person – it's just that once the fantasy fades, reality hits differently.

Getting stuck on someone – especially when it's limerence – is often driven by uncertainty, and by deeper unmet attachment needs. So when that uncertainty suddenly disappears – when the person becomes emotionally available – the intensity of your feelings can fade too. The power of it drops away because what was feeding it isn't there any more. I've seen this happen so many times. Someone spends months (or even years) pining for a person who finally turns around and says, 'Okay, I'm in.' And suddenly their feelings shift. Sometimes they disappear altogether. Limerence can also start to ease when you find a secure attachment with someone else, especially if old attachment wounds were part of what fuelled it in the first place. And for most people I've worked with, that's the pattern I've seen underneath it all.

Getting out of limerence, or any kind of fixation on someone, needs a path. A route you can actually follow. And when you do, those intense feelings can start to settle. So here it is; I've laid out an order that generally works well, but this process isn't always as neat and tidy as a step-by-step list. Not every stage will apply to you, and the ones that do might not apply in this exact order. So take your time. Go through them at your own pace, and in a way that feels right for you.

Understanding and accepting it for what it is

The first step in all of this is gently recognizing that what you're feeling might be less about a healthy connection and more of an intense fixation that isn't really serving you. Now that we've explored the difference between healthy connections and the more obsessive, preoccupying kind, you might have a clearer sense of what's really going on for you. The next step is accepting it for what it is. When you start to see that this kind of fixation might be coming from something unbalanced or unmet in you – not from a genuine, mutual connection – it can start to make more sense. It's not really about them being perfect or 'the one'. It's more about how your mind has latched onto them – to fill a void and soothe your pain. Once that clicks, it gets a little easier to step back and see it for what it is – not something you truly want, but something your pain got attached to. What most of us really want is to feel healthy, whole, steady – and that's where our energy deserves to go. Getting clear on that is like laying the first stone on the path forward.

Interrupting the cycle of fixation

Keep an eye on the triggers that pull you back into behaviours that feed your fixation, or limerence – the things that keep it going. These triggers are often emotional. For example, when you feel lonely, it might send you spiralling into thoughts of them – if only they were here, maybe you wouldn't feel so alone. That loneliness might make you check their social media, just to get a glimpse, to feel close in some way, even if it's one-sided. But each time you do that, you only strengthen the pull and prolong the pining. Or maybe you catch yourself comparing your life to friends who seem to have solid, happy relationships. And instead of feeling inspired, you feel like you're the one who's not enough. That feeling can take you back into the fantasy of imagining how perfect things could be between you and this person. Recognizing these emotional triggers is key. Because once you can spot them, you can stop doing the things that keep the cycle going. And that's where your power is – in catching the loop and gently interrupting it.

Distraction can really help too, not as avoidance, but as a way to shift your attention towards something that grounds you. Something that makes it harder for the fixation to take hold. That might be moving your body, listening to music that shifts your mood, reading, calling a friend, walking while listening to a podcast, doing something creative, making plans, tidying a space or spending time with someone. Anything that absorbs your mind enough to give it something else to focus on – something that doesn't pull you back to them.

Interrupting this cycle also means setting clear boundaries with yourself around the behaviours that feed your fixation. This might look like minimal contact, or even none at all, depending on your situation. If you keep getting pulled into looking at things about them, like their social media, and end up feeling triggered, it only deepens the fixation. In those moments, the kindest thing you can do for yourself is step back completely. If setting boundaries feels hard, or if you're struggling to break the habit, try accepting the urges instead of resisting them or reacting in ways that keep the cycle going. Just let them be there, the same way you'd sit with any feeling.

Another powerful way to interrupt the cycle when you feel it starting is by taking a quick physical action – something that pulls you out of it. Physical movement can help regulate your nervous system, it can interrupt rumination, and give you a sense of control when your emotions feel intense. You could try doing ten jumping jacks, running up the stairs, walking around your garden, dancing or even just shaking it off for a minute or two. You can even start seeing your triggers as a fire alarm, something that signals it's time to move and do something else, right then and there.

Interrupting the cycle is a form of self-care. It's choosing your well-being, happiness and healing over the pain your triggers bring. And it's holding onto why that matters. The more space they take up in your mind, the more power they have over your feelings. Breaking that loop is how you take that power back. And when you do, you create space for new experiences and relationships that feel safer and healthier.

Allow fixating thoughts to fade

One of the hardest parts of being hung up on someone is how your mind keeps looping back to them, thought after thought. You can't stop the thoughts from coming, but you can get better at handling them. You can learn to respond differently to them, and when you do they lose that power to pull you back in. When a thought arrives, just notice it and accept its presence. You can say: 'There's that thought about them again.' There's no need to judge it – so no 'Oh, I can't wait for the day we're together!' Just let it be. Don't engage with them. Don't start analysing or building a whole story around them. Simply acknowledge them for what they are, thoughts passing through, no big deal. The more you let them drift by without getting caught up in them, the less sticky they'll feel and their grip on you will start to loosen.

You might also experience thoughts that seem extreme, like, 'They're perfect, and only they can make me truly happy.' Balance this out by recognizing that no one person holds the sole key to anyone's happiness. Is everyone you know really only happy because they get their happiness from one person? Is that where all their fulfilment comes from? No, it doesn't; happiness comes from so many places, not just one person.

There are also future-based thoughts, like, 'My life will be miserable without them.' Try to imagine your future as a wide-open landscape, full of paths you haven't even seen or walked yet. Instead of making predictions based only on the other person, see your future not as a result of them, but as a result of the life you want to live. If they didn't exist, what would you want for yourself? What would still matter to you? Gently guide your thoughts back to your values. For example, if adventure is one of your values, a future thought could be, 'I'm excited for all the incredible adventures ahead, like doing XYZ one day.' Shift your focus to the life that's waiting for you beyond the thoughts about them.

Switch to value-based behaviours

Start paying attention to the automatic behaviours that come with your limerence, pining or fixation – those things you find yourself doing without thinking, even when you know they're not helping. It might be checking their social media, re-reading old messages, replaying conversations in your mind or constantly bringing them up in your thoughts or to others. Once you recognize these behaviours, try naming them. Writing them down can help. Then, for each one, come up with a value-based behaviour to replace it – something that reflects the person you want to be or the life you want to live. For example, if one of your values is harmony, instead of spiralling into fixation, you might focus on activities that bring you a sense of peace. The goal is to start shifting your energy into things that actually move you forward towards what matters.

Reclaim your life

Being fixated on someone else takes up a lot of time and mental energy, and it can consume a big chunk of your life. It can drain your energy and take you away from the things that actually made you feel good. You might have stepped back from hobbies you used to enjoy or social connections that once felt solid. It's important to gently start returning to those things and re-engaging with your life as fully as you can. Take a few moments and jot down what those things were. If nothing really stands out or you don't feel drawn to the old stuff any more, think about what might interest you now – something new that lines up with your interests and the kind of life you want to build. Try to get going again with other things, even if you don't feel like it; start gently, and keep moving forwards. Make space to nurture yourself too. Think about moving your body in ways that feel good, eating food that nourishes you, letting yourself rest and making space to simply pause and breathe – these are the small but powerful ways that remind you how much you matter.

Healing attachment patterns

As I mentioned earlier, attachment patterns can play a big role in unhealthy fixations and limerence, especially when the same pattern keeps showing up with different people. This can be more common for people with anxious attachment styles. I gave you a definition of this attachment style in Part One of this book, where I also described how insecure attachment can shift to an earned-secure attachment over time through personal growth and healthy relationships. You can learn healthier ways of connecting, and a big part of that is understanding and accepting what real healthy connection, validation and security look like. An obsessional fixation isn't that. Sometimes, these fixations are your mind's way of trying to meet an unmet attachment need – or even replaying an old dynamic from earlier in your life. You might find yourself drawn to someone emotionally unavailable, just as someone important was unavailable to you before. When you keep reaching for something that slips away, again and again, it can leave you even more hurt than before.

When you have an anxious attachment, it's not just hard to let go of unhealthy relationships, you can easily fall into seeing the person who hurt you through a softer lens. You minimize their flaws, maybe even try to forget the ways they've let you down. And that makes it easier to stay fixated on them and to keep pining for something that isn't healthy. These attachment patterns can feel oddly familiar, even when they're hurting you. There's something about them that feels known – like, 'at least I understand this kind of struggle'. And because of that, it can be hard to step away from it. Even when part of you knows it's not good for you. Moving towards something healthier can feel like stepping into the unknown. But that's okay, it's how new ground often feels at first. Over time, that unfamiliar place can become the safer one.

If you recognize this pattern in yourself, pause and reflect: is there something you've longed for – something you didn't get in your early relationships? Something you've been hoping another person could finally give you, or complete in you? What is that thing? And how can you give it to yourself now, as the adult you are? If you were healing that part of you, what would you do?

If you want to move towards a more secure way of relating, this is where it starts – meeting your needs in healthier ways. The work you've already done in this book is part of that journey: getting clearer on who you are, understanding your values, setting boundaries, speaking up, letting go of people-pleasing. These are the foundations of earned-secure attachment. And one of the biggest steps is this: recognizing the unhealthy fixations for what they are, choosing to work through them, and gently moving towards something more balanced and real. Because that's what leads you to a steadier connection – first with yourself, and then with others. It might feel uncertain now, but one day you'll look back and see that it was the beginning of real healing.

Build your self-worth

Low self-worth can convince you that you don't deserve any better. So you settle for relationships that hurt, for people who don't really show up for you – because part of you believes that's all you'll get. But it's not. The answer isn't in continuing to shrink yourself to fit into places that make you feel worthless. But the real solution is to start building your self-worth so you can recognize and intentionally choose something better for yourself, and believe you're allowed to want more. The love you have for yourself has to be stronger than your desire to be loved by others. Low self-worth can often be the thing that pulls you towards an unhealthy person in the first place, with the quiet belief that you're only good enough if this person wants you. When you're deep in longing, limerence and fixation it can start to feel like your worth is hanging in the balance, waiting on someone else's validation. You end up chasing that feeling, not getting it and feeling worse – it's a self-perpetuating cycle. Maybe it started with a shaky sense of self. You didn't feel like much to begin with. Then this person came along and, for a second, it felt like they could fix that; being wanted by them would make you feel whole. But when they didn't choose you, or said no, or went silent, it hit that already fragile part even harder. And now you're stuck, hoping the one person who made you feel small is the same person who will make you feel worthy. But they can't, the only person who can do that is you. So try to break that loop, by looking at other places in your life where you matter. Think about the ways you're valuable to others, the things you bring to the table, what makes people grateful for you, and the qualities that make you unique. And don't forget to acknowledge the parts of you that are meaningful on their own, without anyone else needing to validate them. Try to write down one of those things every day, or even just one thing that made you feel good that day, as a reminder that your worth isn't tied to this one person. It could be a small win, something kind you did for yourself or someone else, or a moment where you felt proud. You can make this into a daily practice of connecting with your own value, independent of anyone else's attention or approval. Working on your self-worth isn't just about getting through this phase, it's part of making sure you don't end up here again. It helps you build resilience, so you're less vulnerable to this kind of pull in the future.

Chapter 6: Forgiveness Is About You, Not Them

I couldn't write about moving on from past hurts without talking about forgiveness. And it's something that's come up again and again with the people I've had the privilege of working with. It's not because they're ready to forgive, but because the very idea of it troubles them. There's a feeling that they're being asked to offer some grand act of generosity to someone who's hurt them deeply. It feels so wrong. I hear things like: 'So they get to treat me like that, and I have to forgive them to move on? I'll never forgive them, so I guess I'll never move on.' And I totally get it. It feels like a second injustice, that after everything, this also somehow falls on you. If you've ever felt this way too, you're not alone. You don't have to offer anyone anything if it doesn't feel right.

The way forgiveness is often spoken about doesn't sit right with a lot of people. Especially those phrases we hear everywhere: 'I forgive you' and 'I forgive them.' It makes it sound like forgiveness is all about the other person, and it's something you have to announce. These phrases can also feel like they're being let off the hook, as if what they did doesn't matter any more, like you're handing out a free pass. And when you've been hurt deeply, especially in situations where there's been deep pain, that can feel so invalidating. They did what they did, they made their choices, and they're still responsible for those. You don't owe it to them to say any words if it feels like those words don't sit right for you. And if you do choose to say, 'I forgive them,' let it be because it means something to you – not because you feel pressure, or because it's what people expect.

Because forgiveness can actually be really good for your well-being – both mentally and physically – I want to offer you a different way to think about it.[35] One that's not about them at all. It's just for you. For your healing. Because when forgiveness is done in a way that serves you, it can genuinely help. It can ease the pain, the weight of anger, resentment, anxiety and stress. Not because the other person deserves it – but because you deserve relief. You deserve peace. Holding onto the pain just keeps you chained to it. Forgiveness, in this sense, isn't about letting them off the hook, it's about unhooking yourself. It doesn't mean you're excusing what they did or forgetting it. It means you're choosing not to carry it around any more. That's what this kind of forgiveness is – a quiet, personal act of freedom.

This kind of forgiveness is about helping yourself let go of the replaying, the reliving, the constant turning over of what happened. It frees up your mental and emotional energy so you can start putting it towards what actually matters to you. And maybe the most important part of it involves showing yourself empathy and compassion. It's about you taking back your power, setting a boundary, and deciding that their actions no longer get to shape your emotional world.

So how do you actually do it? Start by asking yourself: 'What does forgiveness mean to me?' It could be any of these things, or something else. Define forgiveness in the way that feels right for you:

- Is it a boundary, a way of drawing a line and saying, I've given enough to this pain?
- Is it the choice to stop carrying something that's weighing you down?
- Is it an inner shift, moving from holding onto hurt to letting yourself feel lighter?
- Is it a way of reclaiming your energy, your time, your emotional space?
- Is it you saying, what they did doesn't get to keep writing the story of how I feel any more?

Once you've defined what forgiveness means to you, so it feels relevant and personal to your experience, you can make a conscious decision to release the hold this person's actions have had on you. You can use daily affirmations for this, like:

'I release the pain they left behind. I choose peace and healing.'
'I'm free from the weight of resentment, I choose lightness instead.'
'I'm reclaiming my energy, time and emotional space – they're not getting any more of it.'

Even small internal affirmations like these can start to shift things, giving you the sense that you're letting the pain float away down a river, drifting off while you stay safely on the bank.

You didn't choose what happened, but you can choose your response. This kind of internal forgiveness is a way of reclaiming your peace. You don't need to tell them you forgive them, you don't really need to tell anyone, it's your choice, and it's your personal boundary. Forgiveness in this way is a quiet liberation – not a reward for someone else's bad behaviour, but a gift to yourself. And from there, instead of dwelling on the injustice, you get to focus on your growth, resilience and values. You get to take whatever lessons you want from the experience and carry them forward, not as wounds but as markers of your strength.

Chapter 7: Getting Closure

Closure. Almost all of us want it. It's like wishing for a clean end to a messy movie, a way to finally put a story to rest. Often, what we're craving in closure is a sense of control over something that feels unfinished or out of reach. But sometimes that closure never comes.

It's completely natural to want it. Deep down, you might be hoping the other person will acknowledge the impact of their actions, really see the hurt they caused. You want to feel understood, like your experience mattered. It's not always about an apology, though sometimes that's part of it too. It's about being recognized, rather than feeling like they just moved on while you're still carrying the weight. At some point, you mattered to them. So when they vanish or minimize the ending, it can feel like they're also erasing your worth, and that really hurts. You might want an explanation from them or their side of the story. But if things have ended, what matters most is how you were impacted. If you feel hurt, then your healing is the priority now. Focus on caring for yourself and learning who really deserves a place in your life moving forward.

Closure might also be your way of trying to make sense of what happened. Wondering if you had a role in it, not just to understand them, but maybe to change something in yourself – or even to change their mind about you. Sometimes we want closure because it feels like the thing that will help us move on. Like we're waiting for a permission slip so we can step forward. For some people, part of that search for closure includes wanting to get back at the person who hurt them. But you don't need revenge. What you need is distance – because that's what creates the space, peace and energy to welcome people into your life who actually deserve to be there.

When closure doesn't come, you might try to find it in other ways. But most of those don't really work. You replay what they said – or didn't say – over and over. You read between the lines, dissect old conversations, analyse their past, their patterns, their personality. You try to label it, make sense of it, wrap it in some kind of explanation that'll make it easier to let go. But often, none of that feels quite right. And even if they gave you a reason, it might not land well with you. It might not be honest, or full, or it might stir up more pain. You might not agree with it or trust it. And then you're right back where you started, still holding the uncertainty of the ending that never came.

So if you're waiting for that perfect conversation, that one final explanation that makes it all click into place, it's okay to stop waiting. Closure doesn't always arrive the way we hope. But that doesn't mean you're stuck. You can close the chapter yourself. You can tie up your own loose ends. That's what internal closure is, realizing that you don't need someone else to give it to you. You can give it to yourself. That's where your power is. When you stop waiting on their words or actions to free you, you start giving that freedom to yourself.

Internal closure is a shift. It's recognizing that you want to feel lighter, and you're ready to move forward, even without every answer. It's deciding that understanding them fully isn't as important as taking care of yourself. That your healing matters more than chasing a reason that might never come.

You might not get closure from them, but you can still get it from yourself. And when you give it to yourself, something important happens. You start trusting yourself more. You realize that you can carry your own endings. That you don't need anyone's permission to begin again, or to move on. Giving yourself closure can involve doing something symbolic: putting away old mementos, closing the mental door, deleting the chat, saying something out loud like, 'I'm choosing to move forward for my well-being.' These small choices help anchor the bigger decision: that you're done waiting, and you're ready to draw the line now. Giving yourself closure can also come with words, like: 'I don't need to understand every detail. I just know this isn't where I want to stay.' It's letting go, even if it wasn't neat or fair or finished. It's saying: 'This is where I stop. This is where I let it be done.' You can create your own words to mark that ending, ones that reflect your experience. From that point, moving forward in alignment with your values becomes your closure too, giving you a sense of direction and the clarity to take your next steps. That's your closure, and you're in charge of it now . . .

Things to hold onto . . .

The hurt that other people cause can stick, and sometimes, when you don't know how to move past it, it doesn't fully fade over time.

That pain might come from betrayal, the end of a friendship or relationship, rejection, toxic behaviour or even unreciprocated feelings – when someone doesn't feel the same way about you. This can also develop into limerence.

Moving past pain is about learning how to interrupt the cycle of fixation – whether it's on them, the hurt they caused or limerence. You can learn how to make those fixating thoughts fade, and switching to values-based behaviours can help you reclaim your life, heal from unhealthy attachment patterns and rebuild your self-worth.

Forgiveness can be part of moving on. It's not about them, though – it's about you asking yourself: 'What does forgiveness mean to me?' It's you finding your own way of drawing the line, saying, 'I've given enough to this pain,' and making the choice to stop carrying something that's been weighing you down.

Closure is something we all want. But sometimes we don't get closure from the other person. Closure can be an internal shift; where you tie up your own loose ends and you close the door.

An Ending and a Beginning

If you've made it here, I want to honour the effort you've put in and thank you for letting me be your guide. Getting here is proof of the work you've done and a sign that you're well prepared for whatever comes next. Not every part of this book will have felt easy, but that's often a sign that we're touching the places where change not only matters most but is needed most. Some chapters might have stirred things up. Others may have landed like a breath of fresh air. And that's the nature of working on yourself. Either way, here's what I hope you'll take away, and come back to whenever you need:

1. Who you are makes sense, even if others haven't seen it yet or don't understand you.
2. You get to shape your life around what you value, not what others expect of you.
3. You are not rejected, some people just weren't for you.
4. You have the right to set limits, it doesn't make you cold; it makes you strong.
5. Your voice matters: speaking up for yourself is part of owning the space that's yours.
6. Looking after yourself lays the foundation for showing up fully for others.

7. You can face hard conversations, you have what it takes to handle them.

8. You can let comparison gently nudge you towards the path you want to follow.

9. No one knows what feels safe to you better than you do, and you have the power to protect yourself.

10. You can heal from hurt and move on with your life, leaving the weight of pain behind you.

You have the tools and the roadmap for all these things now. When you follow that path and use the tools, you'll find your way. So, as you go, keep listening to that part of you, the one that notices, the one that knows, that feels, that needs, that resists and questions – and softens when it's met with the right moments that hold it just as it is.

This may be the end of these pages, but the start of something new is only just beginning . . .

References

Part 1

Chapter 1

1. pp. 7–8 *Research has found that it's not just one gene* . . .
Munafò, M. R., & Flint, J. (2010). How reliable are scientific studies? *British Journal of Psychiatry*, 197(4), 257–8.

2. p. 8 *Research has also confirmed that genes* . . .
Rutter, M., Moffitt, T. E., & Caspi, A. (2006). Gene-environment interplay and psychopathology: multiple varieties but real effects. *Journal of Child Psychology and Psychiatry*, 47(3–4), 226–61.

3. p. 8 *Our environment can influence the way our genes are expressed* . . .
Weaver, I. C. G., Cervoni, N., Champagne, F. A., D'Alessio, A. C., Sharma, S., Seckl, J. R., & Meaney, M. J. (2004). Epigenetic programming by maternal behavior. *Nature*, 430(6992), 178–82.

Chapter 2

4. p. 13 *Their research helped us understand* . . .
Ainsworth, M. D. S., Blehar, M. C., Waters, E., & Wall, S. (1978). *Patterns of Attachment: A Psychological Study of the Strange Situation*, Lawrence Erlbaum Associates.

5. p. 14 *Studies differ in their findings* . . .
Madigan, S., Fearon, R. M. P., van IJzendoorn, M. H., Duschinsky, R., Schuengel, C., Bakermans-Kranenburg, M. J., Ly, A., Cooke, J. E., Deneault, A.-A., Oosterman, M., & Verhage, M. L. (2023). The first 20,000 strange situation procedures: A meta-analytic review. *Psychological Bulletin*, 149(1–2), 99–132.

6. p. 17 *Over my twenty-plus-year career* . . .
Saunders, R., Jacobvitz, D., Zaccagnino, M., Beverung, L. M., & Hazen, N. (2011). Pathways to earned-security: the role of alternative support figures. *Attachment & human development*, 13(4), 403–20.

Part 2

7. p. 35 *The concept of values is well researched* . . .
Matheus Rahal, G., & Caserta Gon, M. C. (2020). A Systematic Review of Values Interventions in Acceptance and Commitment Therapy. *International Journal of Psychology & Psychological Therapy*, 20, 3, 355–72.

Chapter 2

8. p. 39 *For a long time studies have shown how much our values matter* . . .
Ceary, C. D., Donahue, J. J., Shaffer, K. (2019). The strength of pursuing your values: Valued living as a path to resilience among college students. *Stress and Health*, 35(6), 532–41.
Creswell, J. D., Welch, W. T., Taylor, S. E., Sherman, D. K., Gruenewald, T. L., & Mann, T. (2005). Affirmation of personal values buffers neuroendocrine and psychological stress responses. *Psychological Science*, Nov, 16(11), 846–51.
Matheus Rahal, G., & Caserta Gon, M. C. (2020). A Systematic Review of Values Interventions in Acceptance and Commitment Therapy. *International Journal of Psychology & Psychological Therapy*, 20, 3, 355–72.

9. p. 40 *Research has found that living by your values can protect . . .*
Tunç, H., Morris, P. G., Kyranides, M. N., McArdle, A., McConachie, D., & Williams, J. (2023). The relationships between valued living and depression and anxiety: A systematic review, meta-analysis, and meta-regression. *Journal of Contextual Behavioral Science*, 28, 102–26.

10. p. 40 *research has found . . .*
Ceary, C. D., Donahue, J. J., Shaffer, K. (2019). The strength of pursuing your values: Valued living as a path to resilience among college students. *Stress and Health*, 35(6), 532–41.

11. p. 40 *Research also shows that the more people live in line with their values . . .*
Grégoire, S., Doucerain, M., Morin, L., & Finkelstein-Fox, L. (2021). The relationship between value-based actions, psychological distress and well-being: A multilevel diary study. *Journal of Contextual Behavioral Science*, 20, 79–88.

Part 3

Chapter 1

12. p. 61 *Research shows that the brain treats rejection . . .*
Eisenberger, N. I., Lieberman, M. D., & Williams, K. D. (2003). Does rejection hurt? An fMRI study of social exclusion. *Science*, 302(5643), 290–2.

Part 4

Chapter 1

13. p. 87 *Boundaries are about . . .*
McKay, M., Wood, J. C., & Brantley, J. (2019). *The Dialectical Behavior Therapy Skills Workbook: Practical DBT Exercises for Learning*

Mindfulness, Interpersonal Effectiveness, Emotion Regulation, and Distress Tolerance (2nd ed.). New Harbinger Publications.

Chapter 3

14. p. 92 *You risk adopting* . . .
Young, J. E., & Klosko, J. S. (1993). *Reinventing Your Life: The Breakthrough Program to End Negative Behavior and Feel Great Again*. Dutton.

15. p. 93 *Poor boundaries at work* . . .
Rapp, D. J., Hughey, J. M., & Kreiner, G. E. (2021). Boundary work as a buffer against burnout: Evidence from healthcare workers during the COVID-19 pandemic. *Journal of Applied Psychology*, 106(8), 1169–1187.

16. p. 93 *When your work life bleeds* . . .
Pluut, H., & Wonders, J. (2020). Not able to lead a healthy life when you need it the most: Dual role of lifestyle behaviors in the association of blurred work-life boundaries with well-being. *Frontiers in Psychology*, 11, 607294.

Part 5

Chapter 1

17. p. 118 *Research shows that being more assertive can* . . .
ElBarazi, A. S., Mohamed, F., Mabrok, M., Adel, A., Abouelkheir, A., Ayman, R., Mustfa, M., Elmosallamy, M., Yasser, R., & Mohamed, F. (2024). Efficiency of assertiveness training on the stress, anxiety, and depression levels of college students (Randomized control trial). *Journal of Education and Health Promotion*, 13, 203.
Hagberg, T., Manhem, P., Oscarsson, M., Michel, F., Andersson, G., & Carlbring, P. (2023). Efficacy of transdiagnostic cognitive-behavioral therapy for assertiveness: A randomized controlled trial. *Internet Interventions*, 32, 100629.

Eslami, A. A., Rabiei, L., Afzali, S. M., Hamidizadeh, S., & Masoudi, R. (2016). The Effectiveness of Assertiveness Training on the Levels of Stress, Anxiety, and Depression of High School Students. *The Iranian Red Crescent Medical Journal*, 18(1), e21096.

Golshiri, P., Mostofi, A., & Rouzbahani, S. (2023). The effect of problem-solving and assertiveness training on self-esteem and mental health of female adolescents: A randomized clinical trial. *BMC Psychology*, 11(1), 106.

Speed, B. C., Goldstein, B. L., & Goldfried, M. R. (2018). Assertiveness Training: A Forgotten Evidence-based Treatment. *Clinical Psychology: Science and Practice*, 25, 12216.

18. p. 118 *All in all . . .*

Vagos, P., & Pereira, A. (2019). Towards a cognitive-behavioral understanding of assertiveness: Effects of cognition and distress on different expressions of assertive behavior. *Journal of Rational-Emotive & Cognitive-Behavior Therapy*, 37(2), 133–48.

Part 6

Chapter 1

19. p. 140 *Research shows it's all about finding a balance . . .*

Post, S. G. (2005). Altruism, happiness, and health: It's good to be good. *International Journal of Behavioral Medicine*, 12(2), 66–77.

Chapter 3

20. p. 149 *It's been found to affect both men and women . . .*

Duarte, L. M., & Thompson, J. M. (1999). Sex differences in self-silencing. *Psychological Reports*, 85(1), 145–161.

21. p. 149 *Self-silencing has been linked to worse mental health . . .*

Perz, J., Ussher, J. M., Butow, P., & Wain, G. (2011). Gender differences in cancer carer psychological distress: An analysis of moderators and mediators. *European Journal of Cancer Care*, 20(5), 610–619.

Jakubowski, K. P., Barinas-Mitchell, E., Chang, Y. F., Maki, P. M., Matthews, K. A., & Thurston, R. C. (2022). The cardiovascular cost of silence: Relationships between self-silencing and carotid atherosclerosis in midlife women. *Annals of Behavioral Medicine*, 56(3), 282–290.

Part 7

Chapter 3

22. p. 179 *Your values are your compass* . . .

Bechtoldt, M. N., De Dreu, C. K., Nijstad, B. A., & Zapf, D. (2010). Self-concept clarity and the management of social conflict. *Journal of Personality*, 78, 539–74.

23. p. 180 *Understanding and expressing what you need* . . .

Wickham, R. E., Williamson, R. E., Beard, C. L., Kobayashi, C. L. B., & Hirst, T. W. (2016). Authenticity attenuates the negative effects of interpersonal conflict on daily well-being. *Journal of Research in Personality*, 60, 56–62.

Part 8

Chapter 1

24. p. 191 *I'm telling you that it's an entirely natural human tendency* . . .

Kedia, G., Mussweiler, T., & Linden, D. E. (2014). Brain mechanisms of social comparison and their influence on the reward system. *Neuroreport*, 25(16), 1255–65.

Chapter 2

25. p. 193 *So, it's not about avoiding social media* . . .

Meier, A., & Johnson, B. K. (2022). Social comparison and envy on social media: A critical review. *Current Opinion in Psychology*, 45, 101302.

Chapter 4

26. p. 199 *And research shows that the right kinds* . . .
Diel, K., Grelle, S., & Hofmann, W. (2021). A motivational framework of social comparison. *Journal of Personality and Social Psychology*, 120(6), 1415–30.

27. p. 202 *Research shows that social comparison* . . .
Arigo, D., Bercovitz, I., Lapitan, E., & Gular, S. (2024). Social comparison and mental health. *Current Treatment Options in Psychiatry*, 11(2), 17–33.

28. p. 205 *Envy is an unpleasant and painful blend* . . .
Smith, R. H., & Kim, S. H. (2007). Comprehending envy. *Psychological Bulletin*, 133, 46–64.

29. p. 205 *There are two types of envy* . . .
Lange, J., & Crusius, J. (2015). Dispositional envy revisited: Unraveling the motivational dynamics of benign and malicious envy. *Personality and Social Psychology Bulletin*, 41, 284–94.

30. p. 211 *Research shows that people with higher self-compassion* . . .
Neff, K. D., & Vonk, R. (2009). Self-compassion versus global self-esteem: Two different ways of relating to oneself. *Journal of Personality*, 77, 23–50.

Part 9

Chapter 5

31. p. 230 *Gaslighting is a word we've all heard of* . . .

Miano, P., Bellomare, M., & Genova, V. G. (2021). Personality correlates of gaslighting behaviours in young adults. *Journal of Sexual Aggression*, 27(3), 285–98.

32. pp. 236–7 *Blame-shifting is a toxic behaviour* . . .
Smyth, M. R., Teicher, S., & Wilde, D. J. (2023). How does denial, minimization, justifying, and blaming operate in intimate partner abuse committed by men: A systematic review of the literature. *Trauma, Violence, & Abuse*, 25(3), 1853–70.

Part 10

33. p. 260 *This might lead to* . . .
Willmott, L., & Bentley, E. (2015). Exploring the lived-experience of limerence: A journey toward authenticity. *The Qualitative Report*, 20(1), 20–38.

Chapter 5

34. p. 274 *This is like blaming* . . .
Gehl, K., Brassard, A., Dugal, C., Lefebvre, A. A., Daigneault, I., Francoeur, A., & Lecomte, T. (2024). Attachment and breakup distress: The mediating role of coping strategies. *Emerging Adulthood*, 12(1), 41–54.

Chapter 6

35. p. 288 *Because forgiveness can* . . .
Mróz, J., & Kaleta, K. (2023). Forgive, let go, and stay well! The relationship between forgiveness and physical and mental health in women and men: The mediating role of self-consciousness. *International Journal of Environmental Research and Public Health*, 20(13), 6229.

Index

acceptance
  Acceptance and Commitment Therapy (ACT) 35
  compliments and 131–2
  conflict and 176, 182, 187, 198
  healing from the pain caused by others and 271, 275, 276, 278–80, 283
  parenting styles and 22
  people-pleasing and 138, 147, 149
  rejection and 55, 57, 60, 61, 64, 66–8, 76, 77, 81, 82, 84
  self-comparison and 208, 210
  toxic behaviour and 232, 233, 235, 238, 239, 253, 255
  values and 41, 43, 50
accommodator 173–4
action
  change and 50–51
  personality and 11
  values and 48–51
agreeableness 12, 119, 143, 146
aggressor 173–4
Ainsworth, Mary 13
anxiety 20, 29, 40, 75
  anxious attachment styles 14–15, 283–4

assertiveness and 116, 118, 123, 135
boundaries and 86, 89, 93
comparison and 190, 195, 201, 207, 209
  conflict and 167, 168, 171, 172
  healing from the pain caused by others and 265, 274, 283–4, 288
  people-pleasing and 142, 144, 146–7, 148, 152, 154, 156, 165
  toxic behaviour and 221, 242–3, 249, 250, 254
appearance, comments on 126
assertiveness 11, 14, 29, 43, 48, 49, 115–35, 155, 219
  body language and 132, 133
  defined 117–18
  difficulty with 119–20
  how to be assertive 121–36
    1. Know the needs you want to assert 121–2
    2. Phrases for everyday life 122–7
      appearance, comments on 126
      behaviour. uncomfortable 125
      borrowing money/material items 126

assertiveness – *cont.*
   food or service, unhappiness with 126
   interrupting 124–5
   no, saying 123–4
   opinion, expressing a different 125
   personal information shared without consent 126
   perspective, questioning of your 125
   pressuring you, someone is 126
   refunds 126
   rudeness 124
   words misinterpreted 125
  3. Building your confidence 127–9
    Stage 1 – The foundation 128
    Stage 2 – Stepping up to address common everyday situations 128–9
    Stage 3 – Increasing assertiveness 129
    Stage 4 – Advancing your assertiveness 129
  4. Broken record technique 130–31
  5. Embrace compliments assertively 131–2
  phrases that convey insecurity 134
  respectful, clear and direct, assertiveness as 133
  speaking, confidence and 134
attachment styles 5, 13–17, 18, 23, 31, 64, 246–7, 257, 261, 278, 283–5, 294
  anxious attachment 14–15, 283–4
  avoidant attachment 14, 15
  earned-secure attachment 14, 15–17, 31, 283, 284
  exploitative attachment 246–7, 257
  healing attachment patterns 283–5
  secure attachment 14, 278
authenticity 30, 35, 81, 142, 146, 180, 196, 226
authoritative parenting 18–20
authoritarian parenting 18, 19
avoidant attachment 14, 15
avoider 173–4

behaviour, uncomfortable 125
betrayal 27, 260, 261, 264, 265, 294
blame
  blame-shifting 236–8, 257
  conflict and 168, 179, 184, 186
  parenting styles and 22
  rejection and 78
  self-blame 274
  shifting 236–8, 257
  toxic behaviour and 227, 231–2, 236–8, 248, 257
body language 250
  assertiveness and 132, 133
  boundaries and 103
  conflict and 178, 183–4, 186
borrowing money/material items 126
boundaries 2, 14, 25, 85–113, 129
  conflict and 170, 177, 178

cost of living without 92–4
defining and setting your
   95–108
   1. Know your needs and build your boundaries 95–100
   2. Find your way through your feelings 100–101
   3. Ditch the auto YES! 101–2
   4. Boundary-setting visualization 102–4
   5. Body boundaries 104–6
   bonus boundary phrases 106–8
definition of 87–8
difficulty setting 89–91
digital/technology boundaries 97, 99
emotional boundaries 86, 96, 98
healing from the pain caused by others and 257, 280, 284, 288, 289, 290
material boundaries 96, 99
mental boundaries 96, 98–9
parenting and 19, 20, 21
people-pleasing and 140, 146, 149, 150, 155, 157, 160, 164
physical boundaries 86, 96, 97, 98
reactions to your 109–12
relational boundaries 96–7, 99
self-comparison and 201–4, 216
time boundaries 96, 98
toxic behaviour and 217, 219, 228, 233, 234, 236, 237–8, 244, 248, 252, 253
trauma and 28–9
values and 50

Bowlby, John 13
broken record technique 130–31

change 3
awareness and 5
personality and 9, 11
possibility of 17, 253
smallest actions leading to 50–51
understanding as first step to 4
closure 3, 260, 273, 291–3, 294
comparison 1, 2, 30, 61, 189–216, 243, 298
   choosing healthy self-comparison 199–215
   1. Compare yourself using your values 199–201
   2. Create boundaries around self-comparison 201–4
   3. Turn envy into advantage 204–7
   4. Tame negative self-comparison thoughts 207–9
   5. Process your emotions 209–11
   6. Choose compassion over criticism 211–13
   7. Focusing on gratitude instead of others 213–15
cost of unhealthy comparison 195–8
defined 191
origins/causes 192–4
Six Steps to Emotional Calm 210–11
compassion 2, 22, 43, 66, 70, 74–6, 84, 110, 179, 228, 271

compassion – *cont.*
  criticism and 211–13, 216
  moving on with 255–6
  self-compassion 66, 74–6, 84, 211–13, 271
communication skills
  assertiveness as 117, 118, 121, 122, 135
  boundaries and 86
  conflict and 169, 173, 175
  gaslighting and 232, 234
  identity and 19, 20, 24
  parenting and 19, 20
  people-pleasing and 138
  rejection and 74, 78
  toxic behaviour and 238, 250
compliments 131–2, 251
conflict 2, 23, 25, 167–88, 197, 219, 254, 273
  assertiveness and 117, 119, 123
  defined 169–70
  handling with confidence 175–87
    1. Own your feelings 175–7
    2. Draw your lines 177–8
    3. Use your values 179–80
    4. Understand what you want or need 180–81
    5. Listening 181–3
    6. Body language and voice 183–4
    7. Finding your higher ground 184–6
    8. Recognize everyone's truth 186–7
  overwhelming, why conflict feels so 171–4
    accommodator 173–4
    aggressor 173–4
    avoider 173–4
    communication skills 173
    conflict traps 173–4
    insecurity and anxiety 172
    overwhelming emotions 171–2
    passive-aggressor 173–4
    past experiences 172–3
    people-pleasing and 138, 140, 141, 142, 143, 145
    trauma and 29
    triggers 169–70, 175, 182, 185
    values and 39–40, 48, 54, 179–80
connection 2, 13, 15, 23, 43, 44, 49, 61, 62, 66, 117, 197
  moving on and 273, 276, 278–9, 282, 283, 284
  rejection and 76–7, 81
  toxic behaviours and 233, 234, 238, 240–41, 246, 252
conscientiousness 143, 144
courage
  pain and 267, 271
  personality and 10
  rejection and 79, 82
  values and 43, 49
creativity 9, 43, 280
culture, identity and 5, 7, 23–6, 31

digital/technology boundaries 97, 99

earned-secure attachment 14, 15–17, 31, 283, 284
emotional boundaries 86, 96, 98
emotional shape-shifting 244–6, 257

empathy 263, 288
  boundaries and 91, 111, 112
  conflict and 170, 182, 184
  people-pleasing and 143–4
  personality and 12
  secure attachment and 14
  toxic behaviour and 223, 232, 233, 248, 254, 257
  values and 43
envy
  comparison and 196–7, 200, 204–7, 209, 210, 216
  toxic behaviour and 248, 251
exploitative attachment 246–7, 257

feelings
  boundaries and 100–101
  'Feel Your Feelings' method 69–70, 100–101, 157, 171–2, 265
  owning your 175–6
  personality and 10–11
  processing 68–70, 77, 84
  unreciprocated 261
fixation, cycle of 277–85, 294
  allowing fixating thoughts to fade 281–2
  interrupting 279–81
food or service, unhappiness with 126
forgiveness 43, 287–90, 294

gaslighting 228, 230–34, 236, 248, 257
genetics 5, 7–8, 31, 203
  epigenetics 8
gratitude 43, 49

focusing on 213–15, 216
guilt 2, 265
  boundaries and 90, 93, 100, 101, 110, 111, 115
  comparison and 214
  healthy 156, 157, 159
  people-pleasing and 150, 155, 156–60, 164, 165
  unhealthy 157–60

harmony
  people-pleasing and 143, 154
  values and 43, 48, 282
healing attachment patterns 283–5
healing from the pain caused by others 259–94
  betrayal and 260, 261, 264, 265, 294
  can't move on, what to do when you 273–86
  closure 291–3
  fixation, cycle of 277–85, 294
  forgiveness 287–90, 294
  friendship/relationship, end of 262
  healing attachment patterns 283–5
  limerence 260–64, 271, 273, 275, 278, 279, 282, 283, 285, 294
  painful thoughts, taking power out of 266–9
  processing your emotions 264–5
  reclaiming your life 282–3
  rejection and 261, 262, 264, 273, 294

healing from the pain – *cont.*
  roots of your pain, understanding 261–3
  self-worth, building 285–6
  taking back the wheel 270–72
  toxic behaviour and 262
  understanding and accepting it for what it is 278–9
  unreciprocated feelings and 261
  value-based behaviours, switching to 282
honesty
  assertiveness and 117, 135
  closure and 292
  conflict and 179, 261
  pain and 261
  people-pleasing and 152
  personality and 11
  toxic behaviour and 224
  values and 37, 41, 43

identity
  attachment and 5, 13–17, 18, 23, 31
  genetics and 5, 7–8, 31, 203
  parenting and 18–22, 23, 31, 234
  people and culture and 5, 7, 23–6, 31
  personality and 5, 7–12
  temperament and 5, 7, 31, 64
  trauma and 27–31
  independence 15, 19, 44, 49, 239
  insecurity 25, 29, 34, 86, 144, 265, 283
  comparison and 193, 194, 195, 197, 200, 201, 205, 207, 209–11

conflict and 172, 182, 185
insecure attachments 14–16, 31
phrases that convey 134
toxic behaviour and 223, 235, 242, 251
interrupting 86, 124–5, 129, 138

joking, hostility and 247–8, 251

learned behaviour 142, 145–6, 165
limerence
  pain caused by others and 57, 260–63, 264, 271, 273, 275, 278, 279, 282, 283, 285, 294
  rejection and 57
listening, power of 181–3

material boundaries 96, 99
mental boundaries 96, 98–9

no, saying 2
  assertiveness and 123–4, 132, 135
  boundaries and 104–6
  identity and 24, 25, 28
  people-pleasing and 144, 156, 157, 160
  rejection and 59, 60, 62
  values and 46, 49, 50
opinions, voicing 107, 125, 129, 143, 146, 149
overwhelming emotions, conflict and 168, 171–3, 177, 179, 188

parenting 18–22, 23, 31, 234
  authoritative 18–20

authoritarian 18, 19
permissive 20–21
uninvolved 18, 21–2
passive-aggressor 173–4
past experiences 3, 16, 22, 28
   acceptance and 67
   assertiveness and 119, 121
   boundaries and 91, 104, 105
   comparison and 193, 203, 209, 211
   conflict and 168, 172–3, 177, 178
   judgement and 228
   moving on from 273-86, 287, 294
   people-pleasing and 29, 142, 151
   rejection and 77
   toxic behaviour and 223, 227, 228, 237
   trauma and 28, 29, 30
patience
   identity and 10
   people-pleasing and 152–3
   self-compassion and 75
   toxic behaviour and 239, 253
   values and 44, 48
people, identity and 5, 7, 23–6, 31
people-pleasing 29, 49, 137–65, 284
   defined 139–41
   price you pay for 148–9
   stop being a people-pleaser, how to 150–64
      1. Values to stop people-pleasing, using your 150–54

      value of harmony 154
      value of honesty 152
      value of patience 152–3
      value of personal well-being 153–4
   2. Respond differently in people-pleasing moments, how to 155–6
   3. Guilt, free yourself from 156–60
      breaking the cycle of unhealthy guilt 158–60
      healthy guilt 157
      unhealthy guilt 157–60
   4. Self-critical thoughts, dealing with 160–62
      reframing 161–2
   what happens when you stop people-pleasing 163–4
   triggers 140–41, 151–2, 155, 159
   why you're a people-pleaser 142–7
      1. Personality traits 143–4
      2. Trauma 144–5
      3. Learned behaviour 145–6
      4. Fear of authenticity 146
      5. Anxiety 146–7
perfectionism 143, 144, 193
permissive parenting 20–21
personal information shared without consent 126
personality
   people-pleasing and 143–4
   shaping of 5, 7–12
perspective, questioning 125
phrases
   assertiveness 122–7

Index   311

phrases – *cont.*
  boundaries 106–8
  forgiveness 287–8
  insecurity 134
  people-pleasing 155–6
  physical boundaries 86, 96,
    97, 98
  playing hot and cold 238–41
  pressuring you, someone is 126
  projection 231, 235–6, 257

refunds 126, 128, 130, 131
rejection, fear of 2, 25, 28,
  55–84, 89
  breaking free from 66–83
    1. Acceptance 66–8
    2. Process your feelings 68–70
    3. Deal with negative thoughts
      70–74
    4. Stop self-rejecting 74–6
    5. Take comfort in connection
      76–7
    6. Redirection, not rejection
      77–80
    7. Let your values lead you
      past fear 80–83
  defined/explained 59–63
  'Feel Your Feelings' method
    69–70
  healing from the pain caused by
    others and 261, 262, 264,
    273, 294
  origins/causes of 64–5
  people-pleasing and 139, 142,
    144, 146, 148, 165
  personal nature of 78–9
  self-compassion switch 75–6
  reflection for redirection 79–80

thought awareness and reframing
  71–4
relational boundaries 96–7, 99
rudeness 65, 106, 120, 122, 124

second-chance checklist 253–4
secret animosity 251–52, 257
secure attachment 14, 278
self-compassion
  comparison and 211–13
  healing pain and 271
  rejection and 66, 74–6, 84
  self-compassion switch 75–6
  values and 50
self-respect 3
  boundaries and 106, 113
  values and 44, 46, 50, 87
self-worth
  boundaries and 90
  building 285–6, 294
  comparison and 195, 201
  people-pleasing and 148
  rejection and 76
  toxic behaviour and 249
silent treatment 248–50, 257
Six Steps to Emotional Calm
  210–11
social connection 44, 49, 282
speaking, confidence and
  122–7, 134
stability, values and 44, 49

temperament 5, 7, 31, 64
thinking/thoughts
  fixating thoughts 281–2
  negative thoughts 70–74, 177,
    207–9
  painful thoughts 266–9

personality and 9–10
reframing thoughts 71–4, 161–2
self-critical thoughts 150,
   160–62, 211–12
time boundaries 96, 98
toxic behaviour 3, 27, 29, 30,
   91, 92, 170, 217–57, 262,
   264, 294
  awareness of 225–6
  behaviours 230–52
   1. Gaslighting 230–34
   2. Projection 234–6
   3. Blame-shifting 236–8, 257
   4. Playing hot and cold
     238–41
   5. Triangulation 241–4
   6. Emotional shape-shifting
     244–6
   7. Exploitative attachment
     246–7
   8. Joking as cover for hostility
     247–8
   9. Silent treatment 248–50
   10. Secret animosity
     251–52
  gut-punch moment 221–2
  motivations for 223–4
  moving on with clarity and
   compassion 255–6
  responsibility for 227–9
  second-chance checklist 253–4
trauma 3, 22, 85, 91, 165
  identity and 27–31
  people-pleasing and 142,
   144–5, 148
  toxic behaviour and 223, 224,
   228, 237, 239, 255
triangulation 241–4, 257

triggers
  comparison 201–3, 209
  conflict 169–70, 175, 182, 185
  people-pleasing 140–41, 151–2,
   155, 159
  rejection 60, 61, 70–71
  toxic behaviour 221, 233, 244,
   275, 279–80
truth, recognizing everyone's
  186–7, 188

uninvolved parenting 18, 21–2
unreciprocated feelings 261, 264,
  273, 294

values 2, 24, 30, 33–54, 101
  action that reflects your 48–51
  alignment with 46–7
  comparison and 199–201, 216
  conflict and 169, 175,
   179–80, 181
  copying and 33–4
  core values, discovering 42–4
  core values, ranking and
   identifying 44–5
  defined 37–8
  defining your 41–5
  goals and 37–8
  harmony, value of 154
  healing from the pain caused by
   others and 270, 282, 284,
   290, 293, 294
  honesty, value of 152
  importance of 39–40
  living by your 46–51
  patience, value of 152–3
  people-pleasing and
   150–54, 165

values – *cont.*
  personal well-being, value of 153–4
  staying connected to 52–3
  values table 43–5

visualization
  boundaries 87, 88, 102–4
  rejection 76
  values 53

Acknowledgements

This book began with the simple act of putting pen to paper, driven by an intention to offer valuable support to those facing challenges. I wrote it with the conviction that what has helped others can help you too. But it's not just me who made this possible. There are so many people to thank who helped bring this book to life, and stood beside me throughout this journey.

Thank you to Eve, my brilliant agent, always there to talk with no question ever too big or too small. To Hockley, your expertise, your calm, your sharp eye and steady presence – thank you for all of it, and for holding the vision of this book with such clarity. Thank you to Lizzy for coming to meet with me at the clinic to explore the very beginnings of this book. Thank you to Jodie for stepping in when I needed. Thank you to Katy for the thoughtful management. To Sian, thank you for your creativity and care, for making things feel fresh and alive. To Amy, thank you for your dedication and hard work in helping get this book into the hands of those in need. And truly, a huge thank you to the entire Bluebird team. Your commitment to my work and its deeper purpose means the world. I feel so honoured to have you all in this with me.

Thank you to my children, for your love and patience. The pride you show in my work is something I hold so close. When I hear you sharing what I do with others, it fills my heart in a way I can't put into words. You've been a constant reminder of why this work matters. Wherever life takes you, always listen for and trust your own voice. There is nothing more important than the truth you carry inside.

My family often says, 'You have a whole team behind you,' especially when things feel like too much. And that couldn't be more true. I want to thank that family team from the bottom of my heart for their unwavering support, not just in everyday life, but through the challenges that surfaced while this book was coming together. I'm also deeply grateful to my friends who stood beside me. To be able to ask for anything and know you'll support me is kindness beyond measure, and your generosity has been an incredible source of strength. Thank you to my wonderful colleagues, after so many years working alongside you, I'm beyond grateful to call you friends.

Thank you to my mother. I am constantly in awe of your grace, and the extraordinary resilience you embody. The way you met life fully, openly, with love and unending acceptance, and the way you kept moving forward no matter what life brought taught me how much strength lives inside us. You inspired me by showing how we endure and overcome, and you motivated me to learn from that strength so I could help others. Thank you to my father for showing me what it means to embody acceptance in the face of whatever comes. You met every challenge with steady resolve. Witnessing your courage, confidence and self-belief has been a gift.

Lastly, I want to thank every single person I've had the privilege to work with over my twenty-two years as a psychologist. We can live our own lives, face our own struggles and gather all the knowledge, skills and clinical training in the world. But without you, I wouldn't have the ever-deepening understanding I bring to helping others day after day. Thank you for trusting me, for showing me how humans suffer and how we heal. It's been a privilege to witness the transformations that have shaped your lives, mine as a clinician and the lives of others who have benefited in turn. That is what this is all about, helping people find their way.

Also by Dr Kirren Schnack

Ten Times Calmer

A handbook of exercises, techniques and advice to take you from anxious to calm by clinical psychologist and TikTok star Dr Kirren.

'If you struggle with anxiety Dr Kirren Schnack has the advice you need.' *Woman's Own*

Available now in paperback.